Faster than the eye

The pictures which a TV screen displays are an illusion, a trick of the eye.

Spots of light

A TV picture is really a tiny spot of light flashing very rapidly across the screen, line by line, over and over again. It takes only 52 millionths of a second to flash along one line. This is too fast for human sight to notice. Any image (picture) that the human brain receives through the eyes takes one tenth of a second to fade, so every part of the screen always seems to be lit up and the picture always appears to fill the screen. The slow-to-fade effect of human sight is called *persistence of vision*. The experiments below prove how the eyes can be tricked.

Light and dark

The brightness of the spot of light varies. It is dim in the dark areas of the picture and bright in the lighter areas. You may like to try making your own picture of lines, divided into dark and light areas, to understand how this effect works on your TV set.

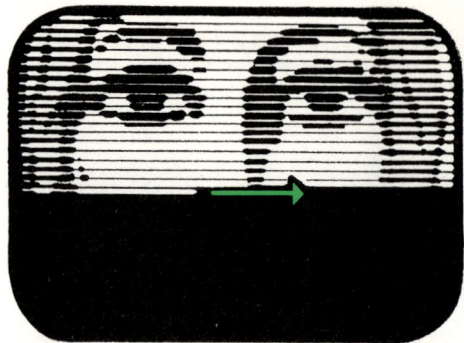

A glowing spot of light 'draws' the picture line by line. In some places it is darker than others. This pattern of light makes a picture.

Whirler

You will need a circle of cardboard, a pen and two pieces of string, each 15 cm (6 in.) long. Draw a fish on one side of the circle. Hold it up to the light and draw a net on the other side so that the fish fits in the net. Make a hole on both sides of the circle. Thread the string through each hole. Tie the ends of the string together. Turn the circle over and over until the string is tightly twisted. Hold the ends of the string taut and let it untwist. See what happens!

Flick-book

You will need a small notebook or 50-60 sheets of paper 10 cm x 7.5 cm (4 in. x 3 in.) stapled together on the left-hand side. Draw a person in the bottom right-hand corner of each page starting at the back of the book. As you work through to the front of the book, slightly change the position of the arms and the legs. When you have finished drawing, flick through the book from back to front. Watch the pictures move!

Television Magic

Television is as exciting behind the scenes as it is on the screen. Find out what goes into making a sports program, a play or a newscast. Learn how pictures and sounds become broadcast signals. And try the projects and experiments that show how some of the illusions you see on TV are created.

The Viking Press   New York

Information stars
A star ★ in an introduction indicates a know-how box on that page. These boxes explain how things work. Look for a star in a box like the one shown here.

Red boxes
Red boxes point out projects to make and quick experiments to try. There are simple instructions and diagrams to follow for each one. All you will need are a few easy-to-get materials.

Contents
2 A window on the world
4 Faster than the eye
6 Remote broadcasts
8 TV camera at work
10 Inside a remote control room
12 From scene to screen
14 Signals around the world
16 Turn on
18 Down on the studio floor
20 Planning a play
22 Behind the scenes
24 Dress rehearsal
26 On location and in the studio
28 Zoom in . . . zoom out
30 Up in the control room
32 Sounds good
34 Looks good
36 Storing TV on videotape
38 Video tricks
40 Take 1!
42 Fitting the pieces together
44 Film tricks
46 Turning film into TV
48 A frame at a time
50 Gathering the news
52 Here is the news
54 Landmarks in TV
56 Not just for fun
58 More and more possibilities
60 Index and glossary

A window on the world

Do you know the meaning of the word television? It comes from the Greek word *tele* which means 'far' and the Latin word *videre* which means 'to see'. It certainly lives up to its name. Turn on a set in America and you can see instantly an event happening in Europe.

Something for everyone

A TV screen is like a magic 'window' on the world through which people see things that are not normally part of their lives. People watching TV share the excitement of the first man on the moon, feel the tension at the start of an Olympic final and see fascinating details of animals living in the wild. Look at any day's TV programs. There will probably be news, cartoons, serials, concerts, comedy shows, dramas, old movies and sporting events to choose from. At the push of a button, the viewer completes the last piece in an expensive jigsaw puzzle which involves thousands of people and millions of dollars' worth of equipment. But how do they make TV programs? What is a frame or a dissolve? Read on to find the answers and learn the amazing way that TV pictures form on the screen.

This book tells you how programs like the ones shown here are made. For example, to find out more about:
animation, see page 48,
remote broadcasts, see page 6,
lighting, see page 34,
making a play, see page 20,
filming, see page 40,
sound and microphones, see page 32.

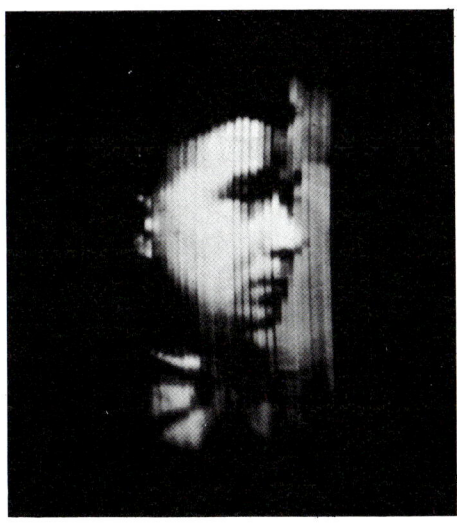

▲ This black and white picture is made up of 405 lines.

◄ This early, fuzzy picture is made up of only 30 vertical lines.

A modern black and white or color picture is made up of 625 or 525 horizontal lines. The more lines there are, the clearer the picture.

A picture of lines

Make your own picture of lines. First trace this pattern and then fill it in following these rules. Start at the top left-hand corner of the 'screen' and work your way across and downward.
1. Always work from left to right.
2. Always start each line by shading in black. When you reach an upright mark stop shading.
3. Start shading again after the next upright mark.

Shade and then stop shading until each line is complete. When you have finished your picture, turn it upside down and look at it from a distance with half-closed eyes.

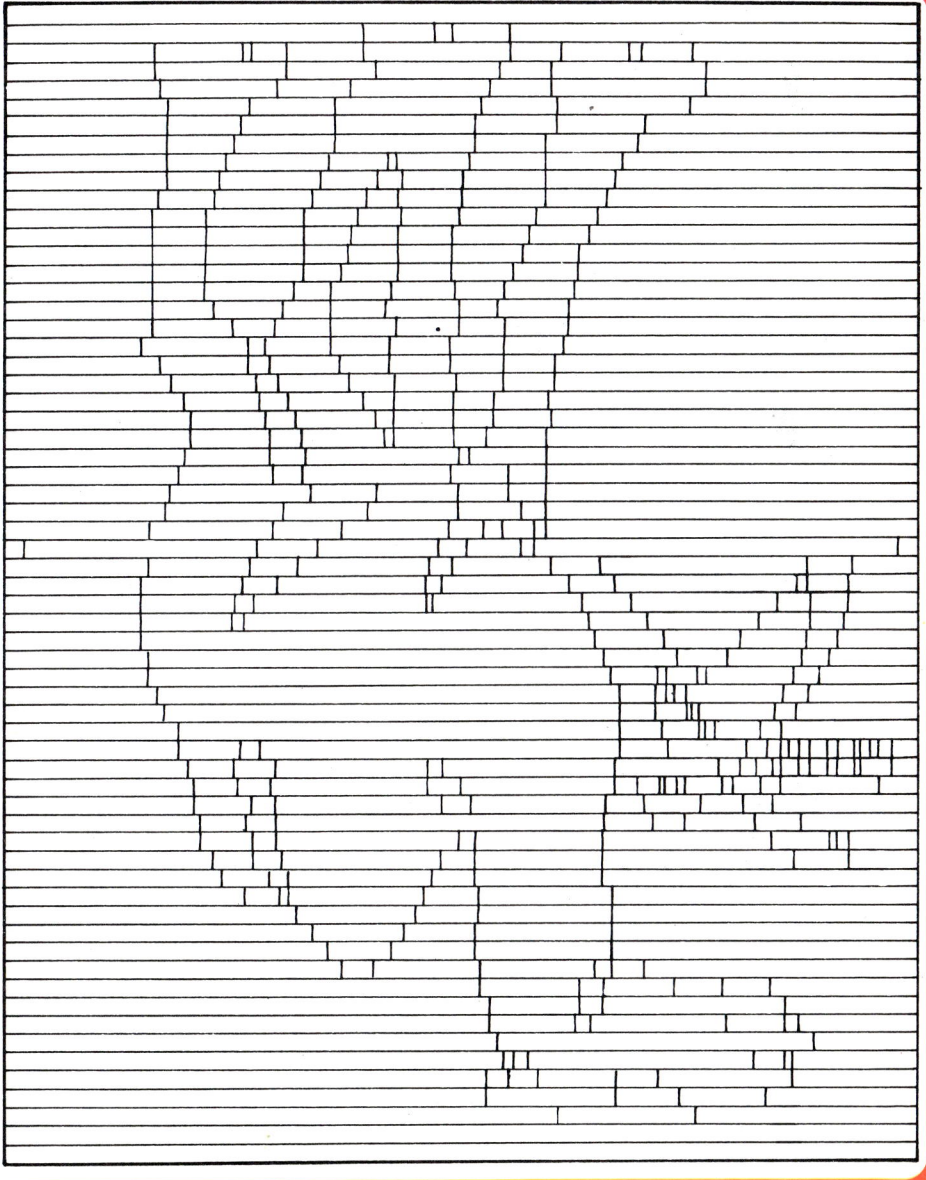

Remote broadcasts

Some of the most exciting television shows are those where TV cameras ★ follow an event that hasn't been specially staged in a studio. The events may be indoor or outdoor, but because the TV equipment goes to the scene, this type of TV program is called a remote broadcast ('remote' for short).

Getting ready

Whenever you watch football games, boxing matches, athletic events, ice capades, concerts and parades on TV, they are remote broadcasts. The most spectacular remote in the world is the Olympic Games. This picture shows the equipment which might be needed at a typical horseracing remote.

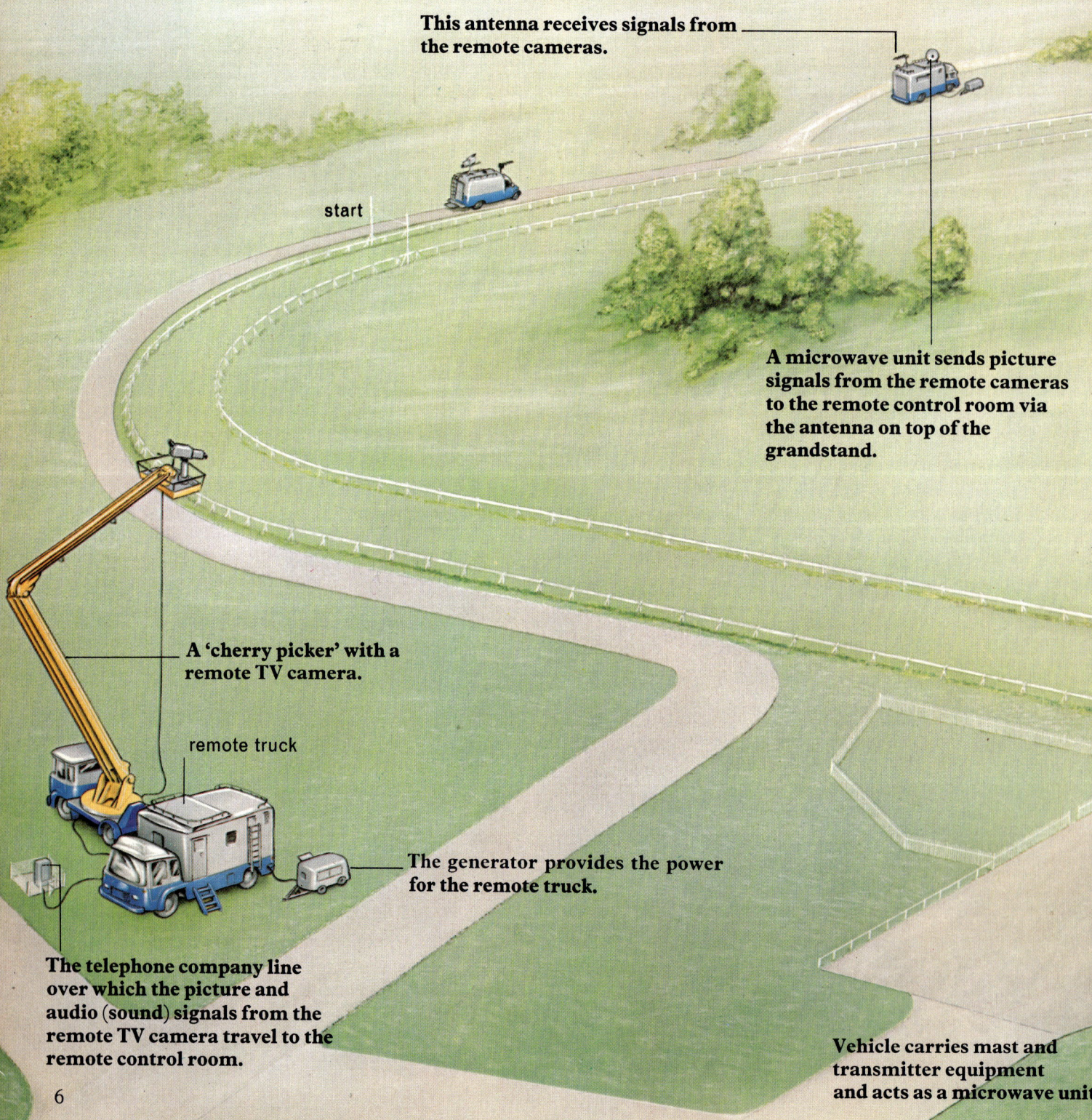

This antenna receives signals from the remote cameras.

start

A microwave unit sends picture signals from the remote cameras to the remote control room via the antenna on top of the grandstand.

A 'cherry picker' with a remote TV camera.

remote truck

The generator provides the power for the remote truck.

The telephone company line over which the picture and audio (sound) signals from the remote TV camera travel to the remote control room.

Vehicle carries mast and transmitter equipment and acts as a microwave unit

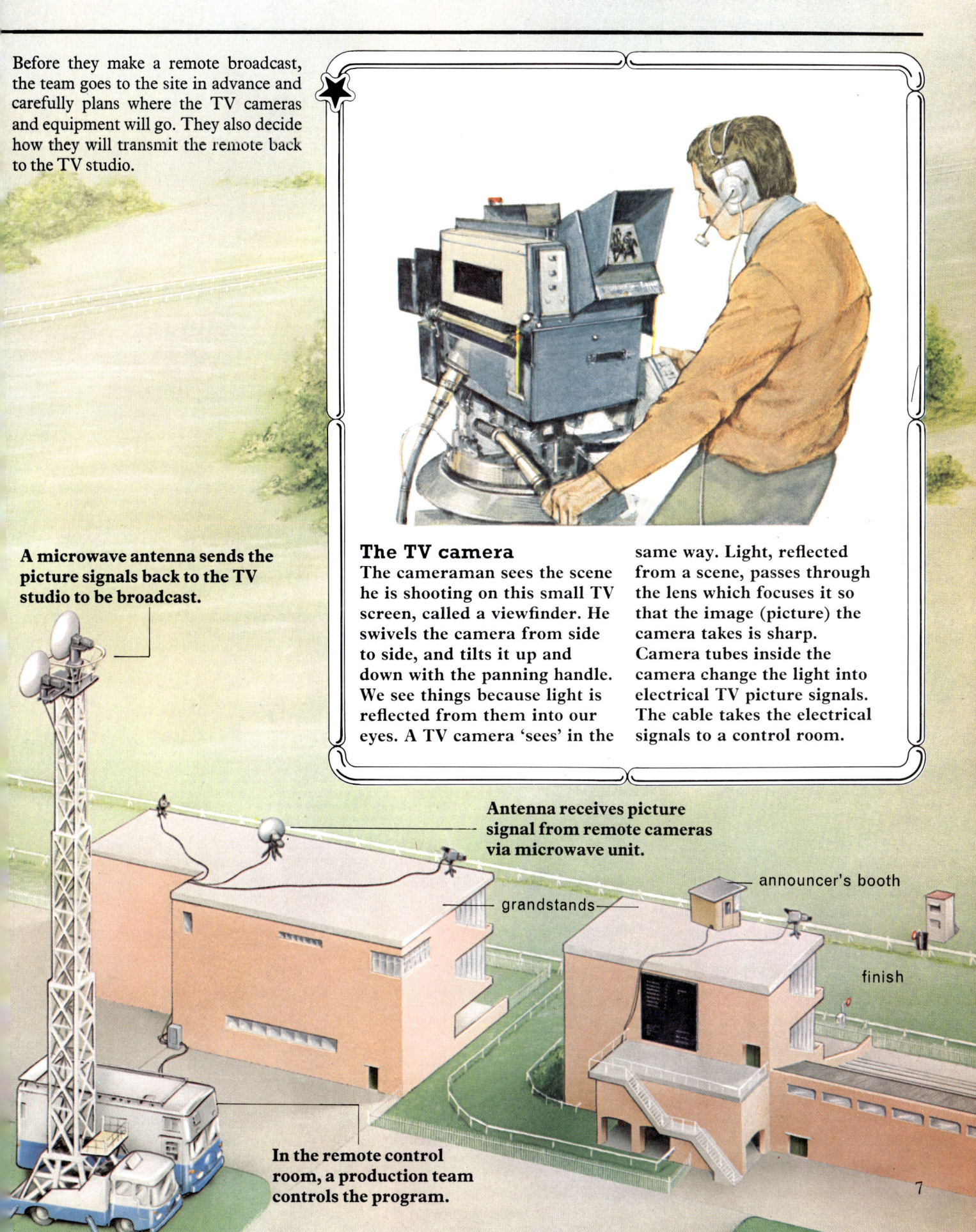

Before they make a remote broadcast, the team goes to the site in advance and carefully plans where the TV cameras and equipment will go. They also decide how they will transmit the remote back to the TV studio.

A microwave antenna sends the picture signals back to the TV studio to be broadcast.

The TV camera
The cameraman sees the scene he is shooting on this small TV screen, called a viewfinder. He swivels the camera from side to side, and tilts it up and down with the panning handle. We see things because light is reflected from them into our eyes. A TV camera 'sees' in the same way. Light, reflected from a scene, passes through the lens which focuses it so that the image (picture) the camera takes is sharp. Camera tubes inside the camera change the light into electrical TV picture signals. The cable takes the electrical signals to a control room.

Antenna receives picture signal from remote cameras via microwave unit.

grandstands

announcer's booth

finish

In the remote control room, a production team controls the program.

TV camera at work

A color TV camera★, like the ones used at a remote broadcast or in a studio, 'sees' a scene in just three colors—red, green and blue. These are the main colors in light, which is really a mixture of colors. (Look at the diagram on the right to see how the colors are mixed to give white light.)

All other colors can be made from various mixtures of the three main ones. So there are no problems in eventually reproducing full color in a TV set.

Splitting the light

The camera has a lens to focus an image of light from the scene, and a system of prisms to bend and separate the light (which travels only in straight lines) into blue, green and red images.

Three camera tubes turn these images into electrical picture signals.

Try the experiments on the next page to help you understand more about light and how it works.

★ **A color TV camera**
Light from the scene is focused by the lens into the camera. A set of special prisms, inside the camera, splits the light into red, green and blue.
Each prism sends an image in one color onto the front of a camera tube. This tube turns the image into electrical signals that become part of the TV signals eventually reaching TV sets.
On page 16 you can find out how these signals are turned back into a picture again inside a television set.

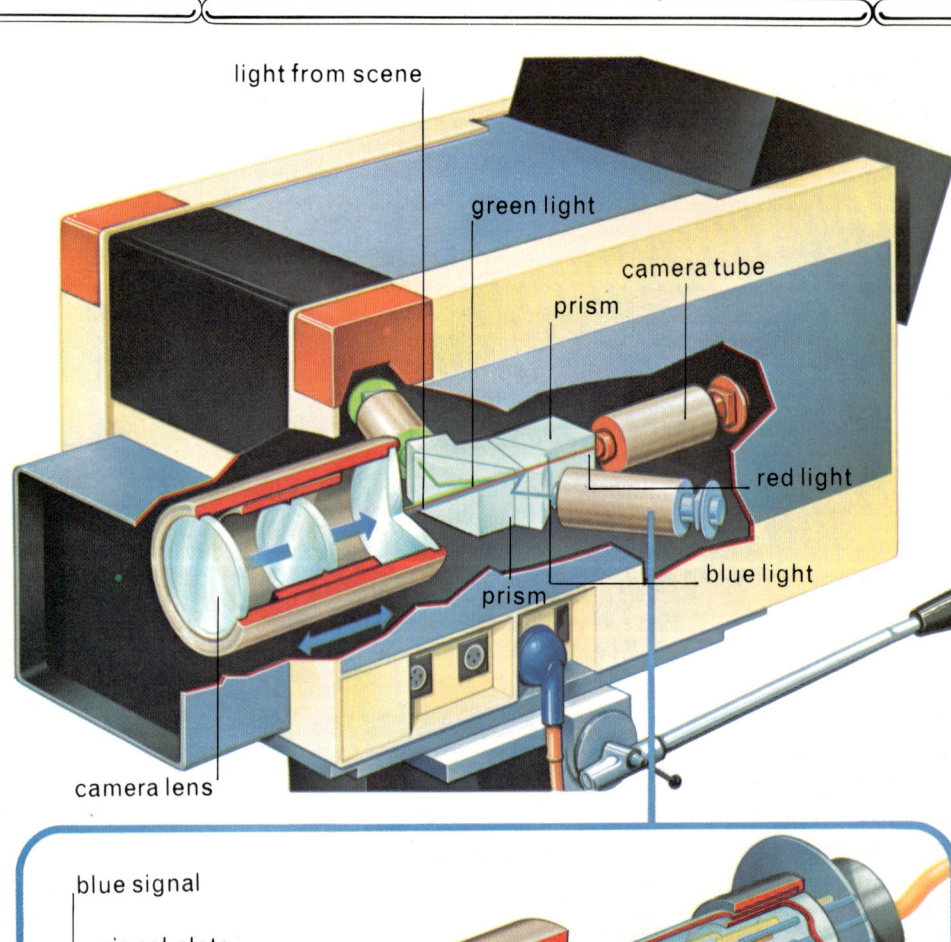

The camera tube
Inside the front of the camera tube is a metal coating called the signal plate. This plate reacts to the brightness of the light falling on it from the image. It allows varying amounts of electricity to pass through it. A 'gun' at the back of the tube fires a continuous 'beam' of electricity at the signal plate. More electricity passes through the brighter parts of the image than through the darker parts.
This is how the picture on the tube changes into electrical signals of different strengths which match the amounts of light from the scene.

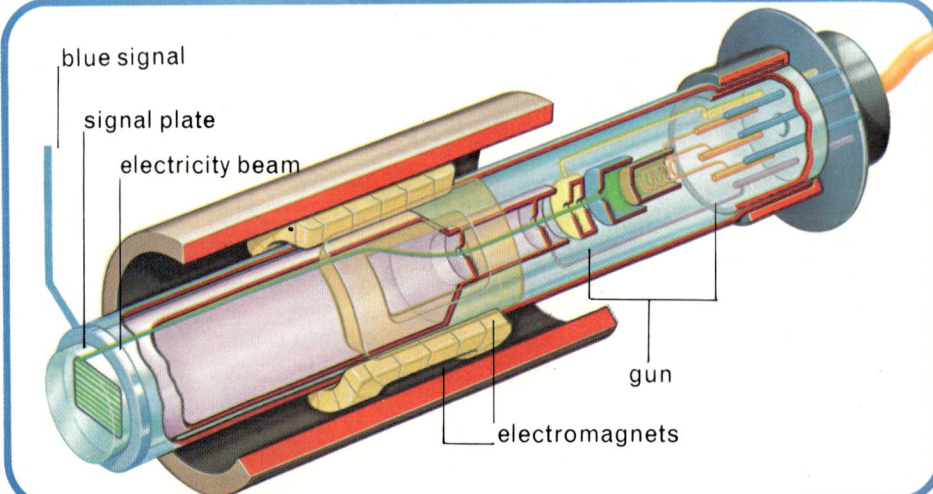

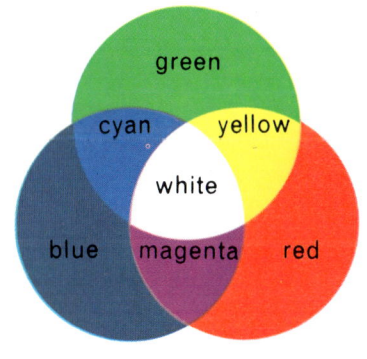

Scanning

Two electromagnets around the camera tube keep the electricity beam on target. One moves the beam from side to side, the other moves it up and down.

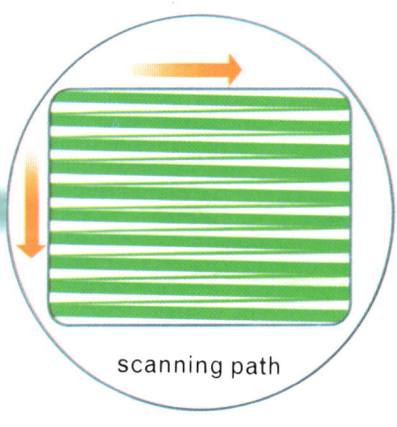

scanning path

In this way, the beam electrically examines the whole image line by line. This movement is called scanning. It is similar to your eyes moving along the page of a book, reading a line and then moving on to the next. When the beam reaches the bottom of the picture, it moves to the top again at lightning speed and starts scanning again. It takes only one twenty-fifth of a second to scan all the lines in the picture.

Three experiments with light

To focus light
You need a magnifying glass and a sheet of paper. A magnifying glass is a lens. Hold it in the sun's rays until you get a bright spot on the paper. This is the focus of your lens. All the rays of light have been bent into that spot. Don't look at the spot for too long and NEVER use the magnifying glass to look at the sun. It will hurt your eyes and blind you.

To reflect light
▶ You will need:
☐ A flashlight
☐ Large and small pieces of black paper and glue
☐ A mirror, modeling clay

Make a slit in the small piece of paper. Glue it over the flashlight. Set up the mirror as shown and shine the flashlight at it along the black paper. What do you notice? Move the flashlight around and watch the light. Try with two mirrors placed at angles to each other.

To see colors in light
▶ You will need:
☐ A flashlight
☐ Several sheets of different-colored cellophane
☐ A piece of white cardboard

Shine the flashlight through one cellophane sheet onto the cardboard. What color light leaves the flashlight? What color falls on the cardboard? Colored cellophane filters out light of colors other than its own. It lets through light of its own color.

Look for colors in light
There are lots of places where you can see different colors in light: through a spray of water on a sunny day, in a soap bubble, in jewelry. All of these things bend the rays of light and we see each color separately. Some colors are bent more than others. Can you tell which?

Inside a remote control room

Have you ever wondered what went on inside the large, closed truck which has cables leading from it and perhaps an antenna and is parked outside a sports stadium or a concert hall? This is known as a remote control room, and it is the control center for a remote broadcast. All the pictures that the cameras take come here through cables and are sent out from here to a TV studio for broadcasting.

Three compartments

There are three main areas inside; one controls sound, another the pictures and the third is a production control room where a director selects which pictures to transmit to viewers' TV screens.

He can choose a picture from one of the cameras or ask for an instant replay★ of a particularly interesting moment. The pictures are sent back from the truck to the TV control room by a signal via a transmitter antenna which is erected on a microwave unit. Instead of a microwave unit, they may use an underground cable (called a land line).

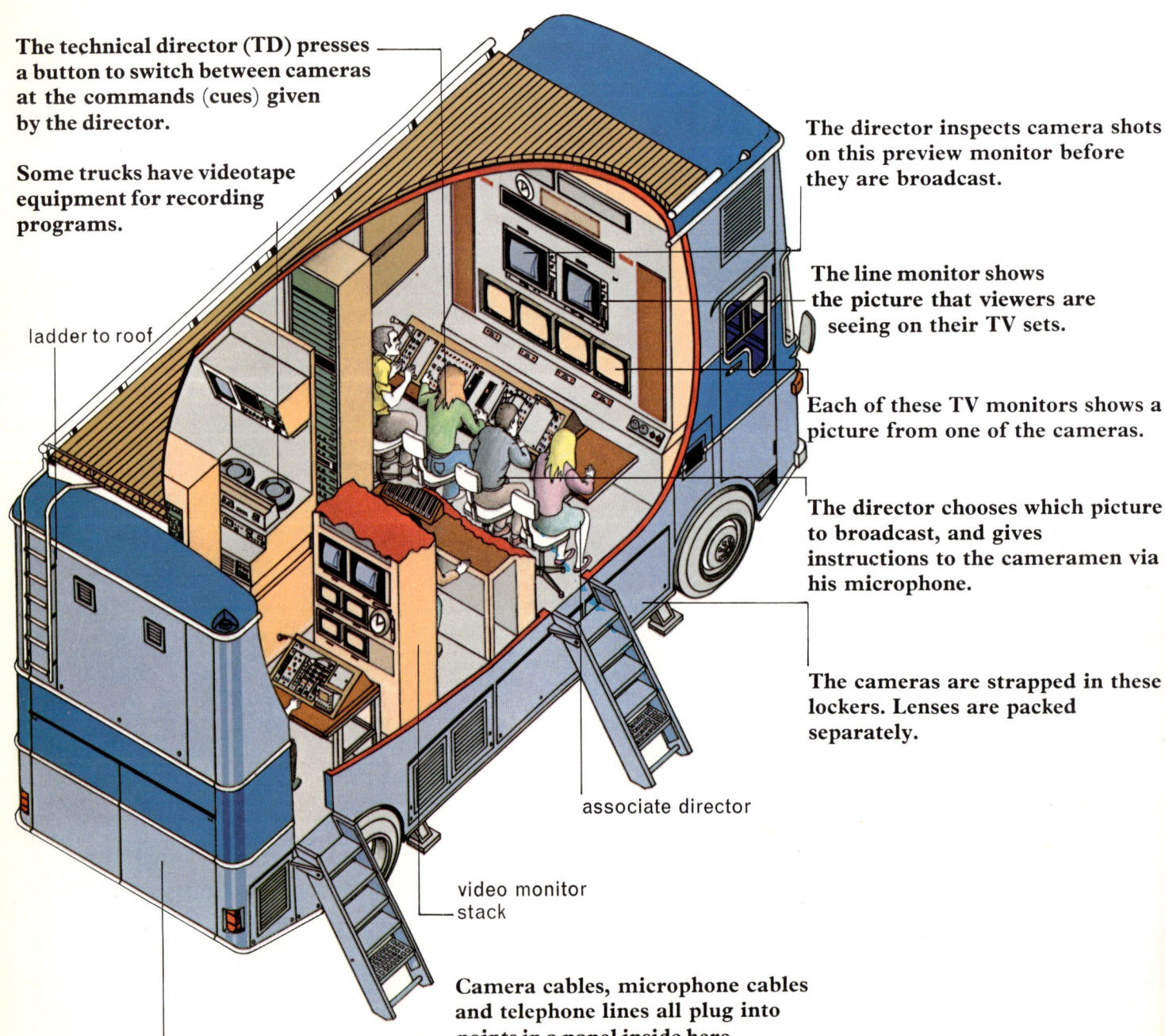

The technical director (TD) presses a button to switch between cameras at the commands (cues) given by the director.

Some trucks have videotape equipment for recording programs.

ladder to roof

associate director

video monitor stack

Camera cables, microphone cables and telephone lines all plug into points in a panel inside here.

The director inspects camera shots on this preview monitor before they are broadcast.

The line monitor shows the picture that viewers are seeing on their TV sets.

Each of these TV monitors shows a picture from one of the cameras.

The director chooses which picture to broadcast, and gives instructions to the cameramen via his microphone.

The cameras are strapped in these lockers. Lenses are packed separately.

The audio engineer controls the volume and balance of the sound at the sound desk.

soundproof walls

sound desk

The roof is strong enough to support a camera and cameraman.

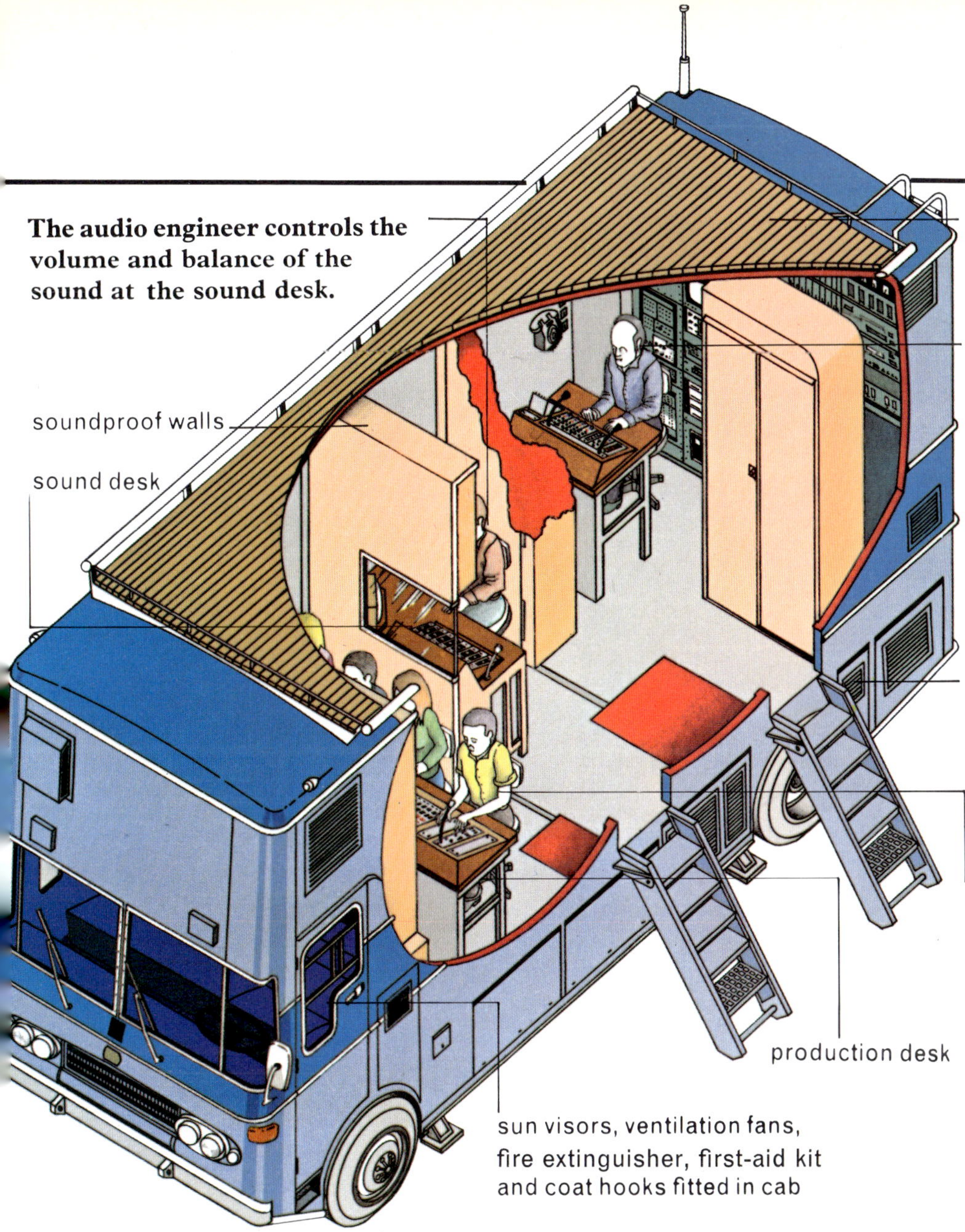

The video control engineers check and control the quality of the pictures on monitors.
The video control monitors are the same as those in the production control area. Engineers match color pictures between the different cameras and adjust for lighting changes, such as when it suddenly becomes cloudy.

If there is a power failure, these batteries keep the sound going until the picture is restored.

The engineer in charge makes sure that the pictures being transmitted are always of high quality.

production desk

sun visors, ventilation fans, fire extinguisher, first-aid kit and coat hooks fitted in cab

---

★ **Instant replay**
Back at the TV control room, video disc equipment can replay an exciting event just after it happens. Two discs are used together. Each side of a disc can hold up to 30 seconds of picture time on hundreds of separate tracks.

Recording
As a disc spins around, the recording head moves along an arm. It records inward on every other track and outward on the empty tracks in between. The heads record all the time the event is happening, wiping out the previous recording each time they go over the same track again. When the director wants a replay of something important, the operator resets the arm at the start of the exciting action in the event. For slow motion each track is replayed more than once—twice for half speed, five times for a fifth of the speed. To 'stop' the picture, the same track is repeated over and over again.

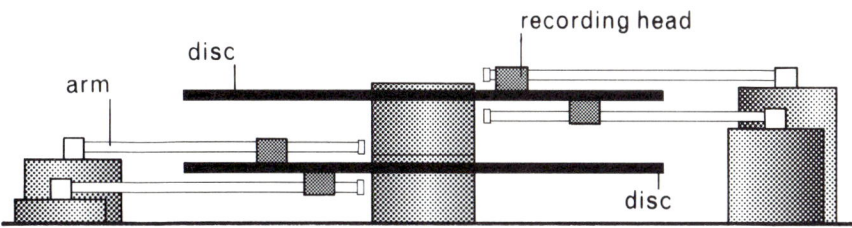

arm, disc, recording head, disc

From scene to screen

A TV camera and the sound equipment split a scene into millions and millions of tiny bits of information in the form of invisible picture and audio signals.

Waves carry signals

Microwave links and cables feed these signals to transmitters and relay stations for broadcasting through the air to thousands of viewers' homes. (This is why people in TV talk about being 'on the air' during a program.) But TV picture and audio signals can't go anywhere on their own, so they travel through the air on *carrier waves* (one wave for the picture signals and another for the audio signals). Carrier waves, which are radio waves, travel at an incredible speed—300,000 km per second (186,280 miles per second). They radiate out continuously from a transmitter, like ripples on a pond when a stone is tossed into it. The waves become weaker as they travel further away from a transmitter, and usually many transmitters are needed to cover a whole country. The areas they cover may overlap so that everyone gets good reception. Remote areas have relay stations instead of transmitters.

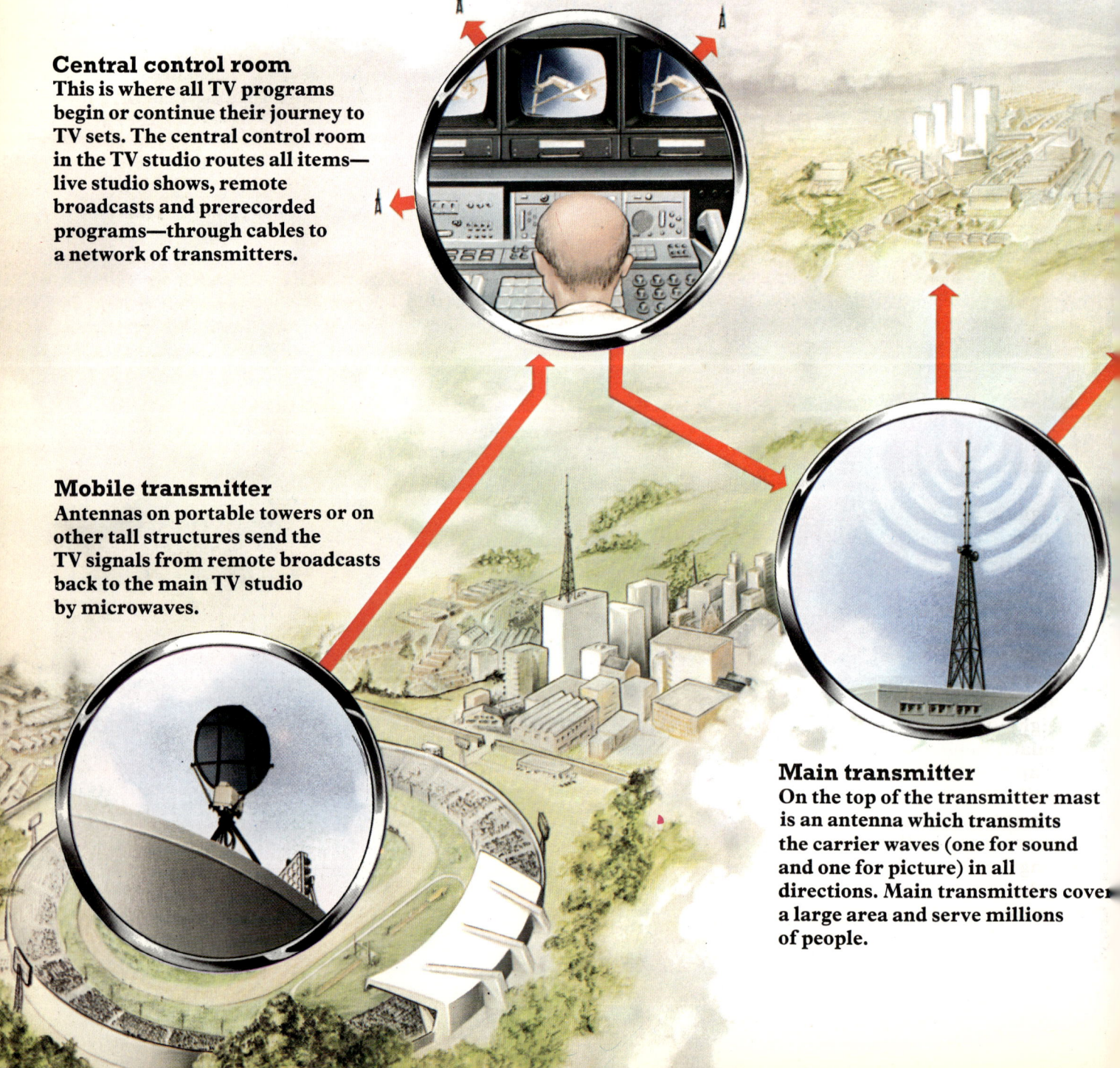

Central control room
This is where all TV programs begin or continue their journey to TV sets. The central control room in the TV studio routes all items— live studio shows, remote broadcasts and prerecorded programs—through cables to a network of transmitters.

Mobile transmitter
Antennas on portable towers or on other tall structures send the TV signals from remote broadcasts back to the main TV studio by microwaves.

Main transmitter
On the top of the transmitter mast is an antenna which transmits the carrier waves (one for sound and one for picture) in all directions. Main transmitters cover a large area and serve millions of people.

Relay stations
Places that are out of range of the main transmitter or that are surrounded by hills or mountains have relay stations. They amplify the carrier waves and broadcast them to villages and small towns nearby. Relay stations cover small areas with a few thousand people.

Antenna on the roof
Finally, an antenna picks up the transmitted carrier waves and passes them along a cable to a TV set. The antenna points toward a transmitter to get strong waves.

The TV set
Inside the TV set, electronic circuits separate the television signals from the carrier waves and change them back into sound and picture for viewers to hear and see.

Transmission problems
The carrier waves travel in straight lines; they cannot bend or curve. If they hit something in their path, it interferes with the transmission, so all the links in the network must keep the waves away from obstacles. Even the Earth's curvature becomes an obstacle to the waves traveling in straight lines. In densely populated countries, there are transmitters about every 60 km (40 miles) apart, near large towns and cities. At each one, the waves are amplified (strengthened) before they are broadcast to viewers' homes on a new carrier wave. In between, relay stations fill any gaps.

Carrier waves bounce off things in the way—buildings, hills, trees.

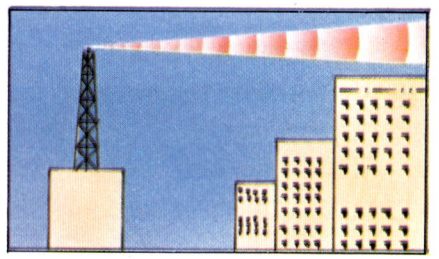

Transmitters are built on tall masts, buildings and hilltops.

Carrier waves cannot follow the curvature of the Earth.

So transmitters are built close to each other to cover most areas.

Signals around the world

Bang! The starter's gun goes and eight swimmers plunge into the pool. All over the world, millions of people share the thrill of this Olympic games final.

Towers in the sky
TV signals broadcast live from the Olympic games have to cross oceans on their journey around the world. But it is not practical to have a transmission network of high towers, rising like giant trees out of the sea. Instead, a 'tower in the sky', called a communications satellite, transmits the carrier waves quickly and clearly over vast distances.

Telstar
A satellite, called Telstar, transmitted the first TV programs from America to Europe and vice versa in 1962. Hundreds more communications satellites have been launched into space by rockets, but only a few are used to transmit TV programs. Most are for international telephone links.

ground transmitting station

Intelsat 4–A
This satellite can relay more than 6000 telephone calls and two TV programs. The antennas on the top always point toward the Earth, receiving and re-transmitting the carrier waves. Thousands of solar cells, covering the black cylinder below, generate electricity from the sun's rays to power the satellite. (It takes a lot of power to amplify the carrier waves.) The lower cylinder spins continuously to keep the satellite steady. Inside the upper cylinder is a battery pack which stores electricity from the solar cells to power the satellite when it is in the Earth's shadow.

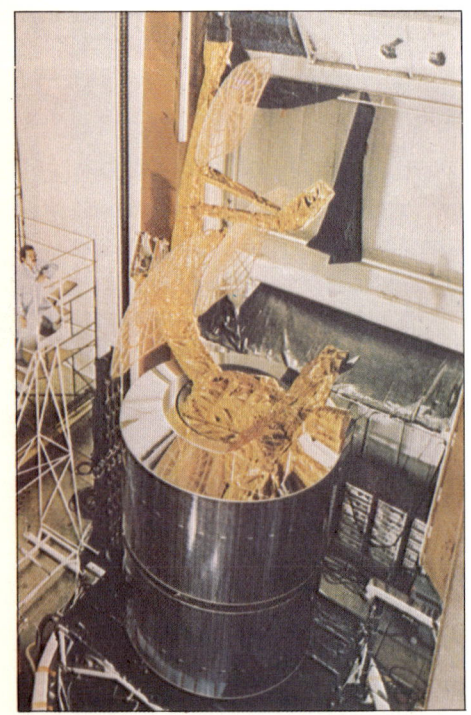

Communications satellite
A satellite orbits Earth, 35,880 km (22,370 miles) up in space. At this distance, it takes 24 hours to travel once around Earth. Since Earth turns on its axis once in this time, the satellite stays in an almost fixed position in relation to Earth.

ground receiving station

Right across the country
Big countries, such as Russia, Brazil and India, use satellites to transmit TV signals from one part of the country to another. In India, where most people live in tiny villages with no schools, the government recently tried a TV satellite experiment. All the programs were educational. Villagers watched programs to help them learn to read and write, grow more and better crops and improve their health and hygiene. Over 5000 villages had a TV set with its own dish antenna—like the one shown here reflected in the water behind the villagers.

Seen via satellite
People in over 100 countries watched events at the Olympic games. The TV signals were sent to Earth stations for transmission to the Atlantic satellite (for the Americas, Europe and Africa) or to the Indian Ocean satellite (for Asia and Australia).

Ground station
A ground station transmits the TV signal carrier waves to a satellite. The satellite amplifies them and sends them back to another Earth station on the other side of the world. A station's dish antenna points directly at a satellite. It can turn or tilt if necessary.

Turn on

One minute the TV screen is gray and empty. Press a switch or turn a knob and within seconds there is sound and a picture. But how does a TV set work?

Look closer

Have you ever looked closely at the screen on a color TV set★? Sit about two feet away and look at one of the lighter parts of the picture, at someone's face, for instance. Can you see that it is entirely covered with a pattern of red, green and blue dots or strips? Now stand back further and look at the whole picture. Can you see the lines across the screen? These are often easier to see on a black and white set. Normally we aren't aware of the dots or lines when we watch a program, but they are always there and are the clue to how the set works.

The drawing shows what happens inside a TV set. *Never touch the controls at the back of a set or try to look inside it because you could be killed by an electric shock.*

Patterns on a TV screen
Look closely at your TV screen. Does it have dots or strips?

The red, green and blue dots are arranged like this.

The red, green and blue strips are arranged like this. Most screens have over one million strips.

The quality of the sound and picture on your TV is partly under your control. You can change the program from one channel to another, make the sound quieter or louder, increase or decrease the color, make the picture lighter or darker, or increase the difference between the light and dark parts.

Too little color

Too bright

Too little contrast

Too much color

Too dark

Too much contrast

16

Secrets of a picture tube

When you switch on, sound and picture carrier waves picked up by the antenna enter the TV. They are amplified and separated from one another. Then the audio and picture signals that started out in the studio are picked out of the carrier waves. The electrical audio signal is amplified and a loudspeaker turns it into the sound you hear. In color sets the picture signal is split into separate signals—one for red, one for green, and one for blue. The color signals are amplified and fed to the color picture tube.

The mask

Behind the screen is a metal plate, called a mask, which is drilled with thousands of holes. Its job is to guide the beams of electricity to the correct colors. Each hole lines up with a group of three dots or strips on the back of the screen. The three beams pass together through a hole.

The guns

At the back of the picture tube are the guns that fire beams of electricity at the screen—one for each color signal. The signals control the amounts of electricity leaving the guns and striking the phosphor dots or strips on the back of the screen. A strong electricity beam makes a phosphor color glow brightly, and a weak beam makes the color glow dimly. The beams scan the screen, line by line.

The faceplate

The front of the picture tube is the screen you watch. It is called the faceplate and the back is covered with red, green and blue dots or strips of phosphor. The electricity beams strike the phosphor colors and make them glow. The dots or strips are so close together that the colors blend, forming the color the TV camera saw originally in that part of the scene.

Down on the studio floor

Through the earphones the production assistant hears the director's voice say, '*Start the clock. One minute studio.*' She tells everyone in the studio to be quiet and to settle down. The director asks the cameras to show their opening shots. The production assistant announces, '*Thirty seconds.*'

The AD (associate director) in the control room calls out a warning, '*Stand by VTR.*'
(The videotape recording engineer is ready to start.)

Good luck, everybody

The AD starts the countdown:
'*Ten, nine, eight, seven, six, five, four, three, two, one . . . . Fade up camera . . .*'

And they're off. This recording is the last stage in making a play which started as a script in the producer's hands months ago.

On the electric studio clock a red light warns when a show is 'on air'.

soundproof doors

A fireman is on duty for scenes in which there is fire.

Lighting technicians angle the lights into position with a pole.

The lights hang from a grid. Each one has a motor and can be wound up and down at the push of a switch on the studio floor.

The boom dolly operator moves the boom operator around the studio.

The floor must be strong and even so that the cameras roll along smoothly.

The PA (production assistant) is director's contact on the studio floor. She passes on instructions and makes sure that everything is running smoothly.

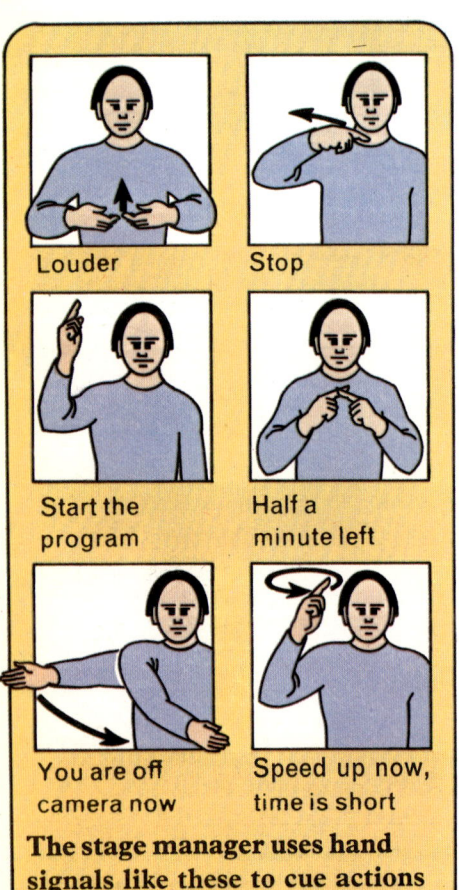

Louder | Stop
Start the program | Half a minute left
You are off camera now | Speed up now, time is short

The stage manager uses hand signals like these to cue actions silently to start or finish or to direct a performer's movements.

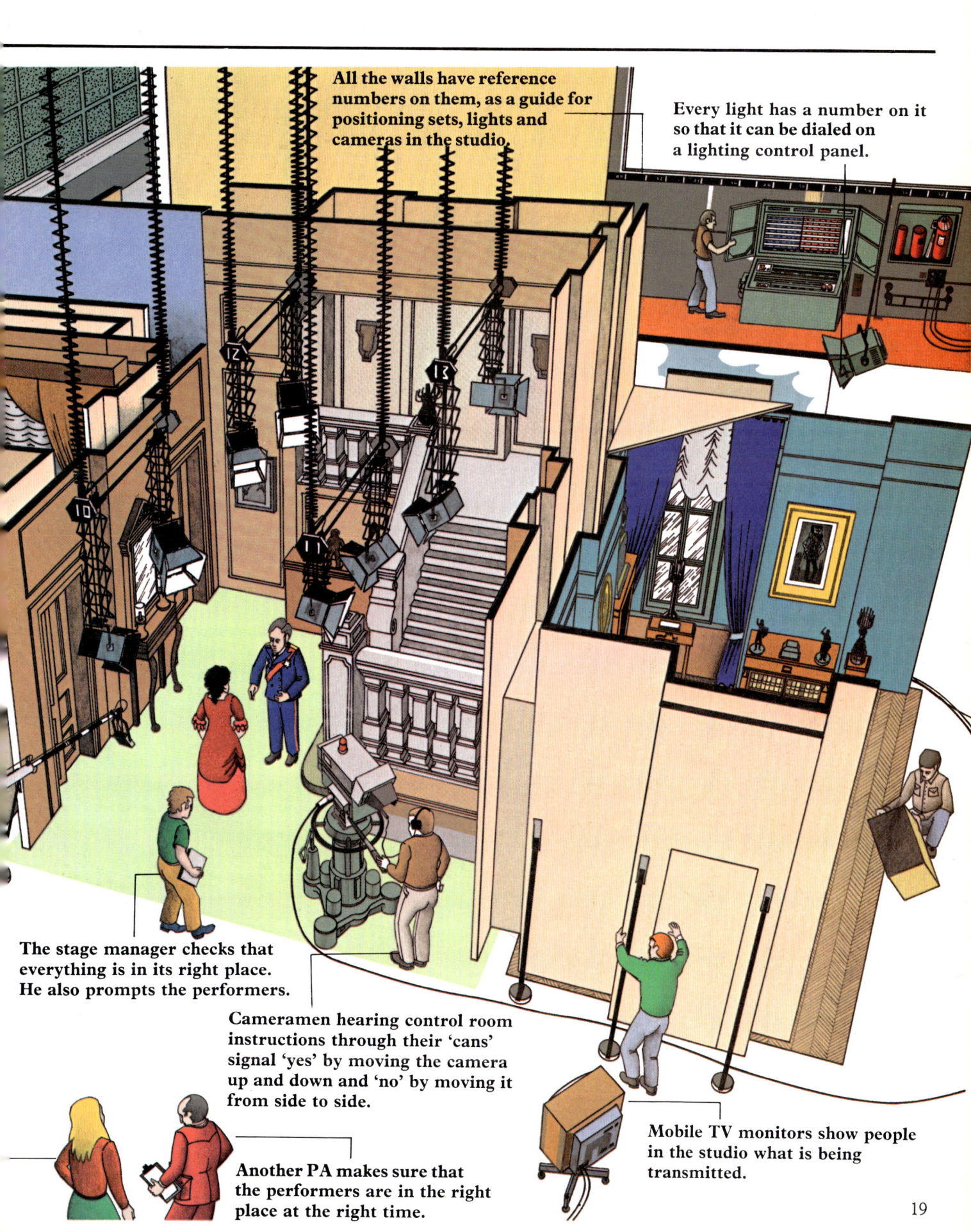

Planning a play

It takes six weeks of hard work and the expertise of about 70 people to prepare a play for recording. Heading the team is the producer, who has overall responsibility for everything. He begins by choosing an interesting script and a director who will make the script come alive for the TV viewers. Then he works out how much everything will cost—the sets, costumes, actors and actresses, props, graphics, music and the pay for the team. (It can cost $100,000 to make a one-hour play.) The producer also discusses the choice of actors with the director, and together they organize the team that works with them.

Creating a play

The director is in charge of the day-to-day work on the program. He or she approves the script, the design, the costumes, the makeup, rehearses the actors and works out the camera shots. The photographs on these and the next few pages show the work that different people do for a typical TV play.

The script

When a writer sends in a script, the producer and script editor read and discuss it. They ask the writer to make any changes or additions they feel are needed. The producer, director and a casting director hold auditions to find suitable actors for the parts.

Designing the set

The set designer reads the revised script and discusses with both the producer and director how the set should look. The designer then makes rough sketches and plans of the set. Sometimes he or she makes up a storyboard (a shortened version of the action of the play, done as a kind of strip cartoon). The set designer also goes with the director to look for suitable film locations for scenes that would be difficult to do in the studio.

This is one of a set designer's rough sketches that act as a base for drawing up more detailed plans. He discusses colors with the costume designer to make sure the set and the costumes don't clash.

The set designer may even make a scale model which shows what the set will eventually look like. This one shows three adjacent rooms.

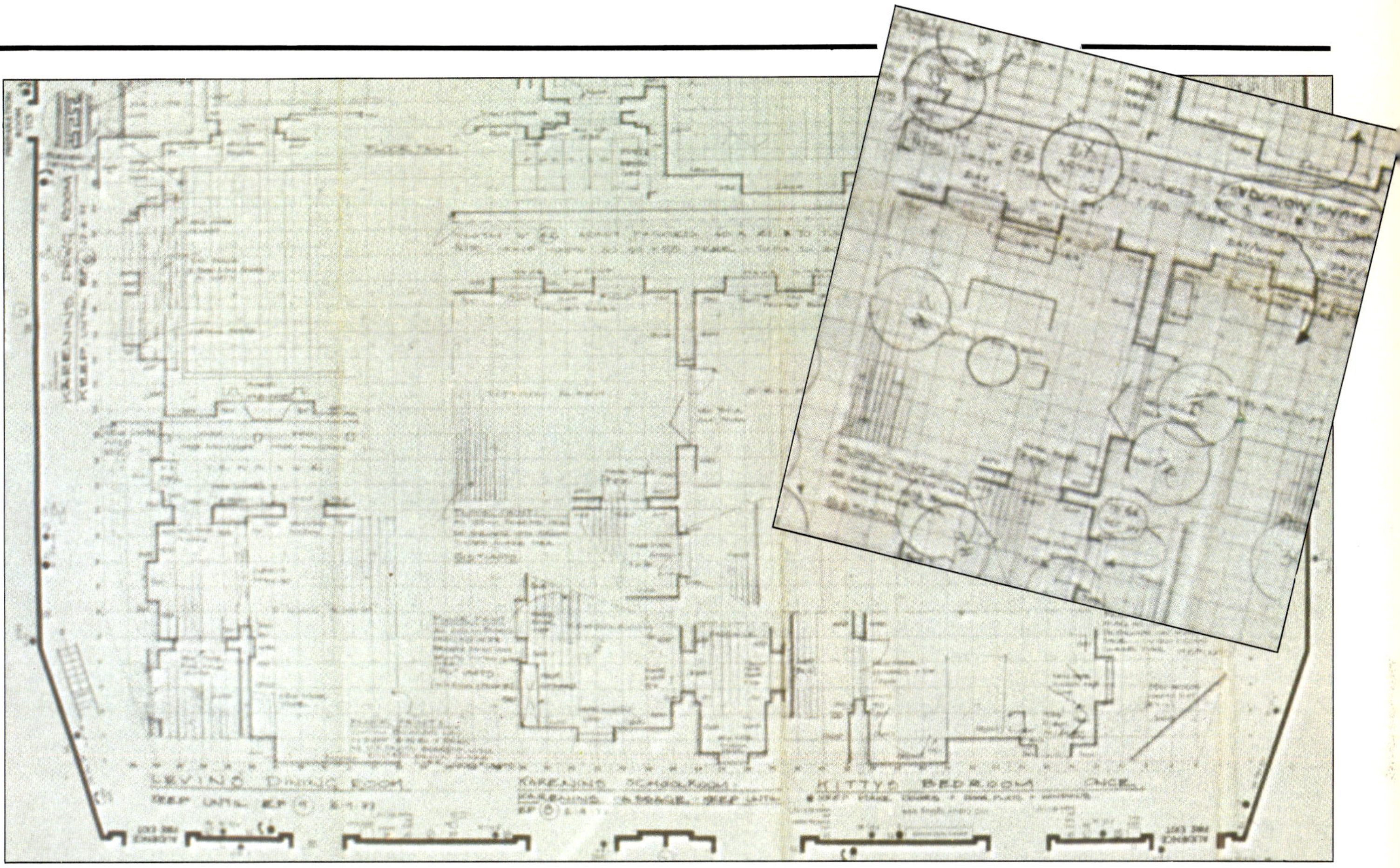

The set designer works out a ground plan of the studio, showing all the positions of places in the set.

It indicates where floors have to be painted and backdrops hung, and where fittings should be built.

After rehearsals, the director marks the positions of cameras and microphones on his plan.

Using the ground plan as a guide, the floor manager sticks colored tape on the floor of the rehearsal room to show the actors where the sets and cameras will be.

The director rehearses the cast and makes notes on his script about the shots each camera will eventually take. The actors and actresses practice their moves and lines.

Behind the scenes

When the studio plan, perhaps a storyboard, sketches and the model are ready, the set designer, costume designer and makeup artist meet the director, the producer, the lighting and audio supervisors and other technicians. They discuss the positions of the cameras, actors, lights and microphones on the set, and sort out any problems.

All set to go
Finally, everyone agrees that the set works. Construction drawings go to the construction workshop, scenic artists begin work on the scenic cloths and the lighting director sorts out the final arrangement of lights. In a large, bare room, the director begins rehearsals with the actors and actresses.

Taking shape
Day by day everything slowly takes shape. In the construction workshop, carpenters measure and cut the parts of the scenery. Some stock pieces, such as plain walls (known as flats), stairs, with two, three or four treads, and columns, come from the storeroom and fit in with the pieces being especially constructed. When all the pieces are ready, they are painted—sometimes to look like bricks or wood paneling—or are covered with wallpaper or burlap.

Finding props
Meanwhile, the prop department, with a long list from the designer, starts searching for suitable props such as furniture, plates, plants, ornaments and lampshades. They find some of the props in their property stores, but unusual things are either hired or bought especially for that production.

The costume designer researches the costume of the period, looking at such details as buttons, hats and fabrics. She draws rough color sketches for all the costumes and buys suitable fabrics.

A graphic designer prepares a title sequence for the play and any other lettering, such as credits. He also designs props—signs, maps, paper money, notebooks and other paperwork.

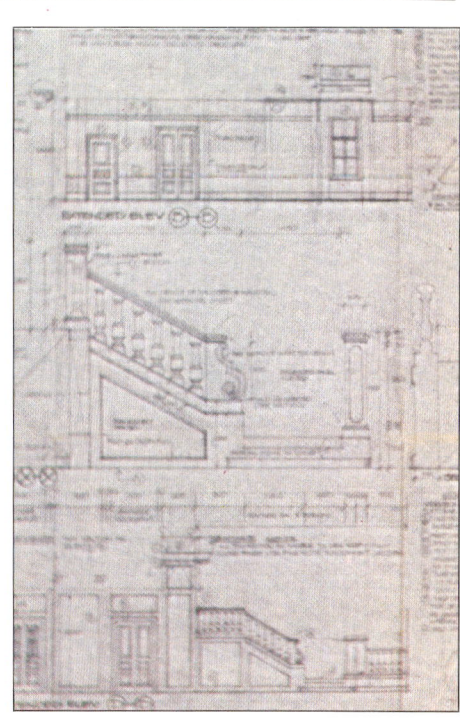

The actors and actresses are measured for their costumes and patterns are made.

Tailors and dressmakers make the costumes, while other wardrobe people find gloves, shoes and bags.

The set designer prepares detailed drawings, called elevations, as a guide for the workshop.

Scenic artists paint enormous backdrops. These are often hung behind a window to show a view of a landscape. The artists may also paint portraits or fakes of famous paintings.

Carpenters build sets in plywood or fiber glass. Walls, staircases and archways are built separately.

Dress rehearsal

The dress rehearsal is in the studio, and it's very important because it is the last chance for things to be changed before the actual recording.

Last-minute changes

Today the cast, wearing their wigs and costumes and fully made up, look like the characters they play. As the actors and actresses perform each scene, the cameras and microphones run through their positions. At the same time, the lighting director checks that his lighting arrangement works well, and the audio technicians listen attentively to the sound balance. Sitting in the control room above the studio, the director watches everything carefully on his monitors—one for each camera recording a shot on the set. He may change an actor's position, move a prop or change a camera angle until he is happy with everything. Set designers, costume designers and makeup artists also keep a constant check on their work during studio rehearsals. Then, at last, it's time for the recording.

The day before the recording, the lights are set in position. Paint machines with patterned rollers prepare the floors. Backdrops are hung up and all the parts of the set are put into position.

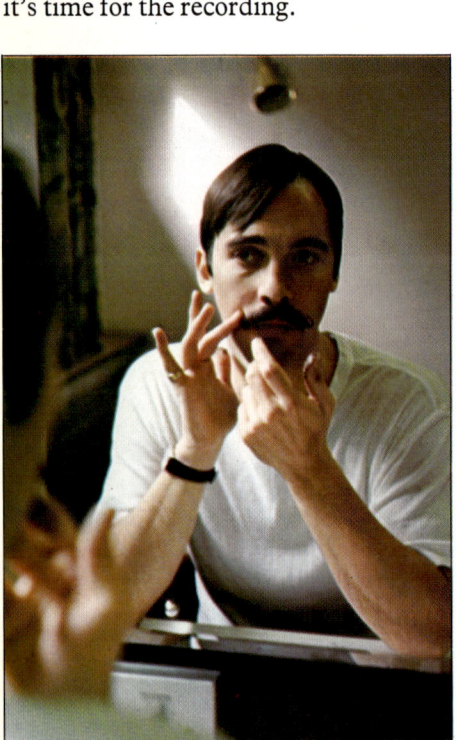

The performers are made up before they put on their costumes.

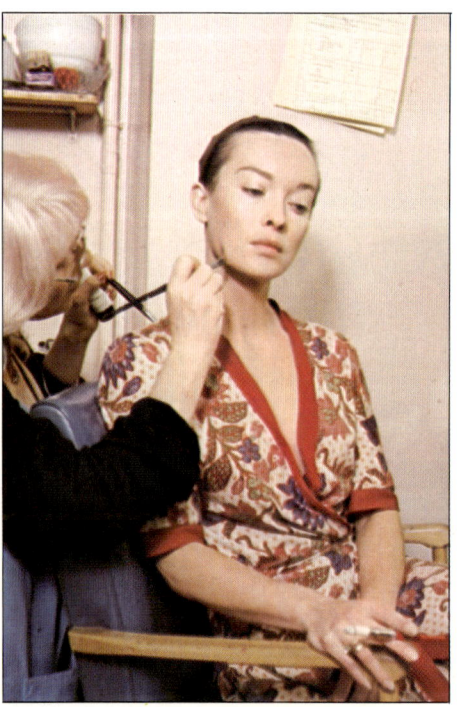

The makeup is put on carefully, to make it look natural in close-ups.

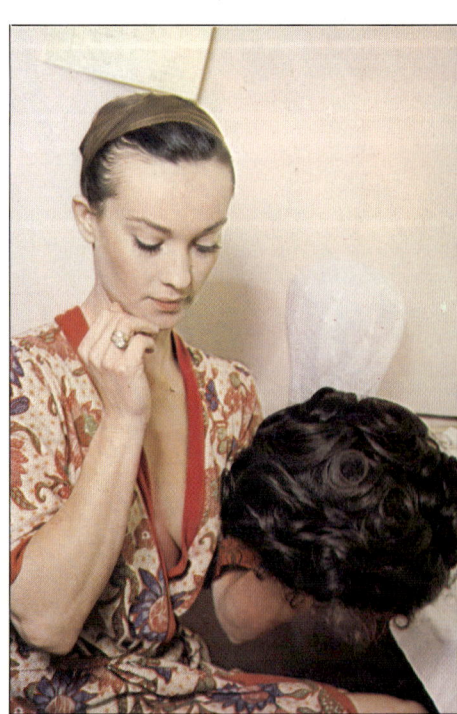

For costume plays, performers often wear very elaborate wigs.

The sets are dressed with drapes and props and final adjustments are made to the lighting.

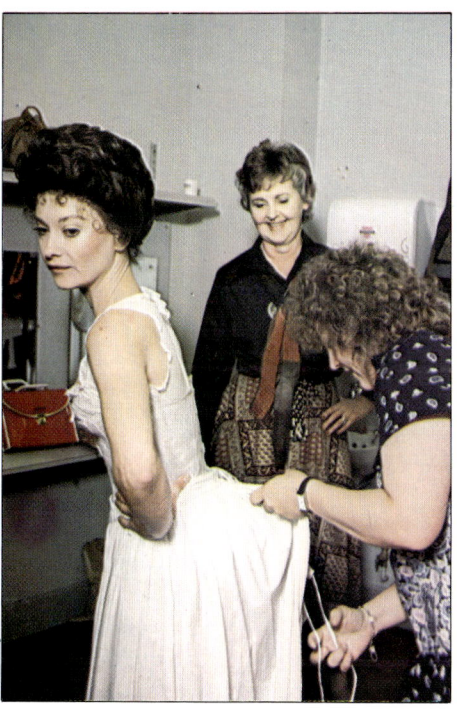

Wardrobe assistants make last-minute adjustments.

These are the three main characters in the drama series based on Tolstoy's novel, 'Anna Karenina', ready for a final recording.

On location and in the studio

Sometimes it is impossible to make scenes in a studio look realistic. Instead, they are shot on film away from the studio in advance of the studio recording. This is called filming on location.

Inside and outside

Some scenes, such as the one here at the racecourse, are shot outside. Others are shot in buildings, such as grand houses or theaters. The film is processed, cut to a specific length and dubbed with sound (see pages 42-43). Before the recording in the studio, the film is laced into a telecine machine. The scenes in the studio are recorded onto a master videotape and the film inserts are also recorded onto it by running the telecine machine at the relevant places in the story. If the film inserts are very long, these are put in the right place in the master tape after the studio sequences have been recorded.

Then when the program is eventually shown on TV, the film and videotape scenes appear as one continuous story.

Real locations have to match scenes shot in the studio and also be practical for filming. Equipment, props, and extra scenery must be transported to the site, and in historical plays, modern office buildings, traffic signs and TV antennas either have to be avoided or disguised. Even for indoor scenes, it may be cheaper to use an actual building to get the right kind of atmosphere and detail.

The pictures here show some of the filming on location and a scene being shot in the studio and recorded. You can see the long boom microphone which picks up the performers' lines. The boom is telescopic and can be wound in and out. A TV monitor shows the picture that is being recorded onto the master videotape.
The director looks at the monitor to check all the camera shots.

Zoom in...zoom out

TV cameramen work as a team. They don't meet the rest of the production team until the day of the studio rehearsal though they may well have worked with some of them on other programs.

Careful planning

All the cameramen normally work to a prearranged plan, prepared by the director, which describes the kind of shots to take and when to take them.

The movements of all the TV cameras★ are carefully worked out by the director to avoid their tangling up cables and crashing into scenery or other equipment on the studio floor.

Though the cameramen don't usually see the shots taken by the other cameras, the director makes sure that they match. He watches the output of all the cameras in the production control room. If the plan hasn't been worked out well, the viewer might see a speaker facing one way in a close-up taken by one camera and facing the opposite way in the wide group shot taken by another. Each camera has a number. In rehearsal the director will often speak to the cameramen by name; but during the recording he calls them by their number.

★ **The TV camera at work**
The light on the top of the camera shines when it is 'on air'. The cameraman focuses the scene he sees on his viewfinder (a miniature TV screen at the back of the camera) by turning the zoom focusing handle in his right hand. On the left side of the camera is a long handle which the cameraman holds in his left hand. With it, he tilts (moves up or down) or pans (moves from side to side) the camera to follow the action. He wears earphones (known as 'cans') to hear instructions from the director. The camera is fixed on a pedestal.

Camera card
This camera card, clipped to the side of the camera, reminds the cameraman of the order of the shots.

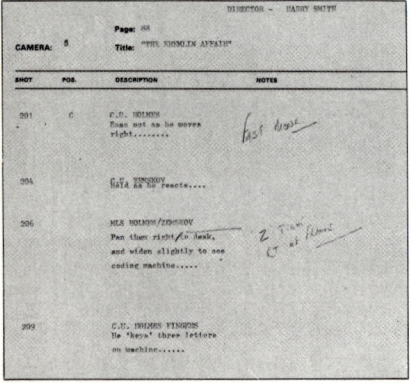

1

2

Zooming in
The cameraman changes shots without interrupting the flow of the scene. He may start by showing the scene, like this (1). Then he zooms in so that the viewer sees only a small part of the scene, like this (2). Everything seems close together. This effect is called foreshortening.

Medium close-up (MCU on script)

Close-up (CU on camera script)

Medium shot (MS on camera script)

Medium wide shot (MWS on script)

Wide shot (WS on camera script)

Choosing the right shot
These pictures show what each type of shot marked on the camera card looks like on a TV screen. The cameraman knows exactly how much of the scene he should show for any particular shot. The director decides which type of shot produces the clearest or most dramatic effect for the viewer. Because TV screens are small, more close-ups and medium shots are used than long or very long shots. When you watch a TV program, look out for changes from one type of shot to another.

Up in the control room

It's the day of the recording and valuable time must not be lost. Up in the darkened production control room, the director and his assistants calmly guide the action on the studio floor below. They sit at a big curved desk which has a panel of buttons and levers on it, and face two rows of TV monitors.

Recording the action

Shots from each of the three cameras appear on the lower monitors and the director, following the camera script, directs the camera movement and tells the technical director when to switch pictures. The AD then calls out the number of the shot to alert the cameraman, and the TD presses the button to record that camera shot.

On either side of the production control room are the video and audio control rooms. In the video control room, the lighting director supervises changes in lighting from scene to scene. In the audio control room, the audio engineers choose which microphones to use and check that they produce natural sound. They also listen for unwanted noises, such as loud footsteps and scraping chairs, and mix in any necessary sound effects.

But it is the engineer in charge sitting with the director who checks the technical quality of the recording. He listens and watches to pick up any imperfections such as a flickering camera shot or a strange noise. If anything goes wrong, everyone starts the scene again.

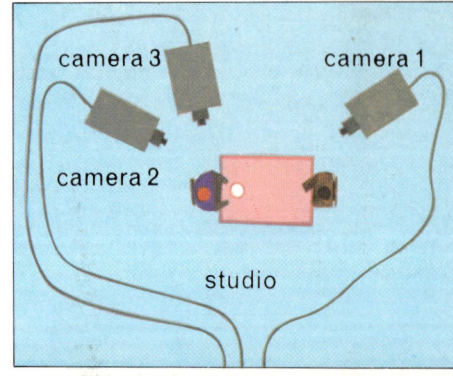

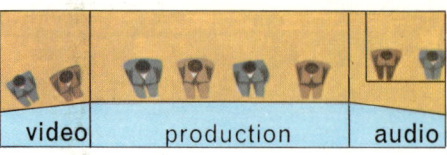

Each camera has a different view of the scene.

Production control room

The director speaks into his microphone. Everyone wearing earphones in the studio and the people in the video and audio control rooms can hear him.

Prerecorded pictures from videotape or telecine machines appear on this monitor.

'Air' sound comes through this loudspeaker.

The line monitor shows everyone the picture that is being recorded at that instant. This monitor shows the same pictures the viewers will see.

The director checks the next shot selected for recording on this preview monitor.

associate director

technical director

engineer in charge

Cuts and dissolves
There are two ways of changing the shots. A cut (1) changes the shot from one camera to another immediately. A dissolve (2) fades out one picture as the next one is brought in. At a certain point both pictures can be seen.

A page of camera script

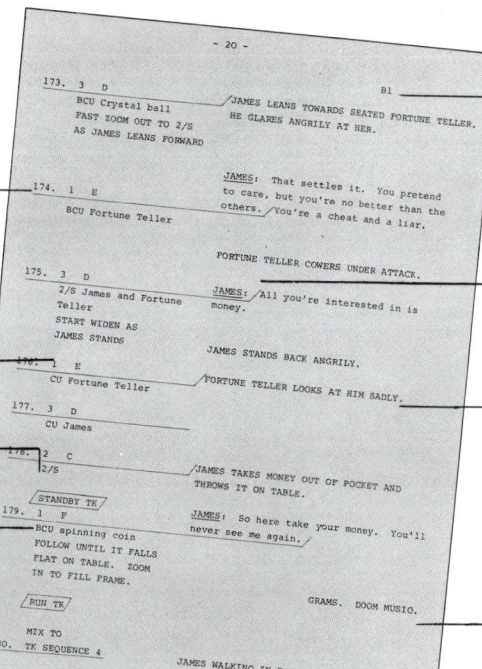

These numbers show each new picture or 'shot' that a camera takes.

This is the number of the camera taking the shot. The letter indicates its position in the studio.

2/S means there are two people in the shot.

These letters describe the kind of camera shot. (ECU means extreme close-up.)

This letter indicates which microphone is being used—the number shows its position.

The line shows exactly the point where the director wants to switch from one camera to another.

Instructions for actors are always typed in capital letters.

Sound effects needed from a tape or disc in the audio control room are marked at the appropriate place.

Camera shots for this script
shots 173-175

Camera 3—start of shot   Camera 3—end of shot   Camera 1   Camera 3

Sounds good

Next time you turn on the TV set, try watching the picture with the sound turned down and see how well you understand what is happening. You will probably find it rather difficult to understand, which proves how important sound is to TV programs. There are always several microphones★ which pick up sound and turn it into electrical signals. They may be slung round the neck, clipped to clothes, hand-held or mounted on the end of a boom.

Picking up sound

In TV it is difficult to record sound because people don't talk directly to the microphone; they move around or talk to another person. Studios can be noisy. During programs technicians move cameras around, change scenery and talk to one another. Audio engineers have to place microphones carefully so that they pick up only sound for the program. The engineers also have to

A microphone on the end of a boom, out of view of the camera, picks up the sound of actors doing a funny sketch. The boom operator can turn it in any direction to pick up sound. He can lengthen or shorten the arm, or move it up or down. The boom dolly has a gear lever, brake and steering wheel.

The audience may watch what is being transmitted to viewers' homes on the TV monitors above them. They hear the sound through loudspeakers.

Microphones, strung down from the lighting grid, pick up audience laughter and applause.

A comedian talks to people in the audience. In the 'warm-up' before recording, the hand microphone is tested.

make the sound realistic for the setting of a scene, whether it is a small room, a country field, or inside a cave or an aircraft. They have records of all sorts of different sounds. Using control equipment, they change the volume of the sound, make it echo, and cut out the bass (deep, low) tones to suit each scene.

Music groups use stand microphones. Each player has a stand with two microphones, one for the instrument and the other for voice. Note the singer's hand mike.

★ How a microphone works

When something vibrates (moves quickly back and forward), such as a plucked guitar string, it produces sound which travels through the air and makes other objects vibrate. You hear sounds because they make your eardrums vibrate, and the vibrations are turned into electrical signals which your brain understands as sounds. Microphones change sounds into electrical signals and have a part similar to an eardrum, called a diaphragm.

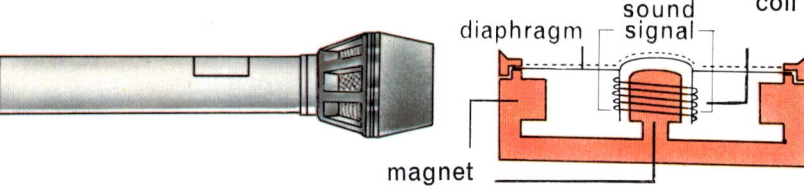

A moving coil microphone has a diaphragm connected to a thin coil of wire placed between two poles of a magnet. Sound striking the diaphragm makes it vibrate, which moves the wire coil. When a wire moves near the poles of a magnet an electric current begins to flow. In this way the sound is turned into electrical signals of varying strengths.

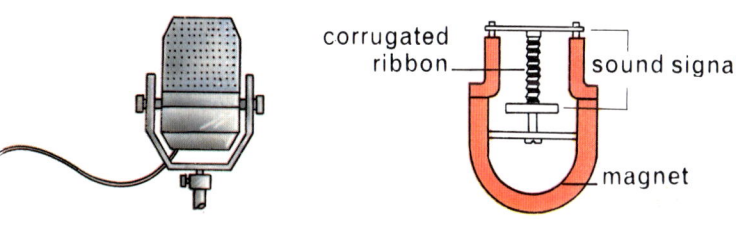

In a ribbon microphone, a thin corrugated foil ribbon is held between the poles of a horseshoe magnet. Sound waves hitting the ribbon make it vibrate between the magnet's poles and this generates an electric current.

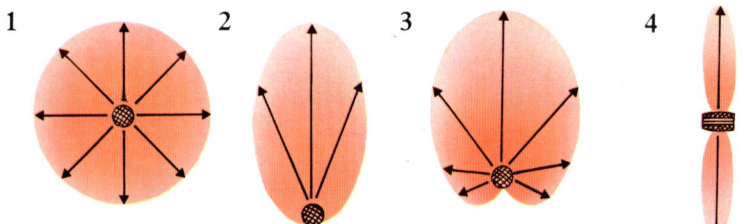

1. Some microphones pick up sound from every direction. They are called multi-directional microphones.
2. A directional microphone picks up sound in front of it.
3. Microphones which pick up sound within a heart-shaped area are called cardoid microphones.
4. Some microphones pick up sound in a figure eight area. These are useful for two speakers facing one another.

Looks good

One day the studio may be set up as a space station on a bright, barren planet and the next day as a gloomy underground escape tunnel from a prison. The amount of light in these two places will be very different and cameras, unlike the eyes, cannot pick out detail in dim light—even dark shots have lighting. To make any scene look realistic through the camera, it depends as much on the lighting as it does on the sets.

100 or more

To produce sharp, lively and interesting pictures, free from unwanted shadows, 100 to 150 studio lights may be used in a drama production. Most of the lights are mounted just below the ceiling, well out of the way, and each one has an identification number. The smallest light, called a 'pup', is ten times more powerful than the average domestic light bulb, but the most powerful are 100 times stronger! There are two kinds of light beam—one which gives a sharp-edged 'spot' of light and the other a fuzzy-edged 'flood' of light. Mounted in front of the lens on some lights, there are hinged flaps, called 'barndoors', which shape the beam.

The lights are fixed to poles which are hung on wires from the ceiling. The poles are raised or lowered by motors, which wind the wires in or out.

The brightness of the lights is controlled remotely from the lighting console in the video control room. Here, the lighting director checks the pictures on the monitors and adjusts the lights by moving levers and pushing buttons.

Try your own lighting

Try some lighting effects of your own in a darkened room. All you need is a strong flashlight. Either ask a friend to hold it for you, or sit in front of a mirror and hold it yourself.

Hold it under your face.

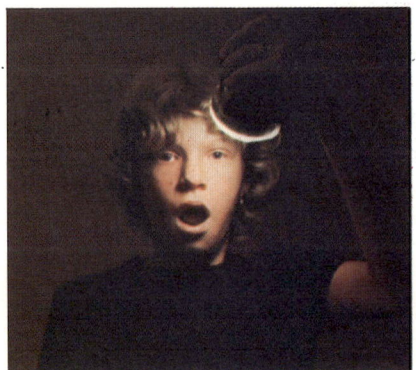

Hold it above your head.

Point it up behind your back.

Point it at the wall behind you.

The lighting plot
The lighting director plans a lighting plot for every production. He makes a chart which shows the position for each light and indicates the kind it should be.

Rigging the lights
Before the final rehearsal begins, the lights are put in these positions. This is called rigging. The angles of lights can be changed with a long pole.
In some studios, the lighting changes for every scene are electronically memorized at the final rehearsal, so that during the recording they are simply switched on by selecting a number on a panel of push buttons.

Lighting effects
It takes at least three lights to make someone look natural. From these pictures you can see how a character looks completely different when the lighting changes.

Soft and hard
There are two main types of light— soft (or fill) and hard (or key). A soft light fills in areas like light on an overcast day. But a scene looks unreal without shadows, and hard lights are needed to cast shadows. Hard light is similar to light on a sunny day.

Storing TV on videotape

In the early days of TV, programs were transmitted 'live' from the studio as they were made. If a dancer tripped and fell flat on her face or an actor forgot his lines or the wall of a studio house fell over, viewers saw it all.

Recorded on videotape

Today, most TV programs are pre-recorded on videotape and any mistakes are removed before transmission. To remove a mistake, an editor used to cut it out of the tape with a razor blade and join the two cut ends, but nowadays editing is done electronically without damaging the tape at all. The machines on which programs are recorded and edited are called videotape recorders, or VTRs ★. These machines are also used to replay a program for broadcasting.

A VTR machine is used for recording, editing and replaying programs.

★ How a VTR works

A VTR records and stores picture and audio signals on magnetic tape, 5.08 cm (2 in.) wide. The pictures cannot be seen on the tape, and a magnetic pulse added to the control track signal on the bottom edge of the tape marks off each whole picture.

Recording

The tape runs from the feed spool past a drum that rotates very fast across the tape. On the edge of the drum are four recording heads which leave an invisible magnetic print of the picture on the tape. The four heads record one after another in narrow bands across the tape. At the same time other heads record audio and guide signals in strips along the tape.

Editing

If there are any mistakes during a recording, the director asks everyone to repeat the scene. This is called a retake. After the recording, an editor removes all the mistakes without cutting the tape by using two VTR machines. The recorded tape is played on one machine and rerecorded on a blank tape on the second machine. When the editor reaches a mistake, he goes past it and records only the retake on the second machine. Pulses on the cue track show him where to start and stop the retake section.
He checks the 'edit' on a monitor.

This editor uses a visual display unit to work VTR machines by remote control.

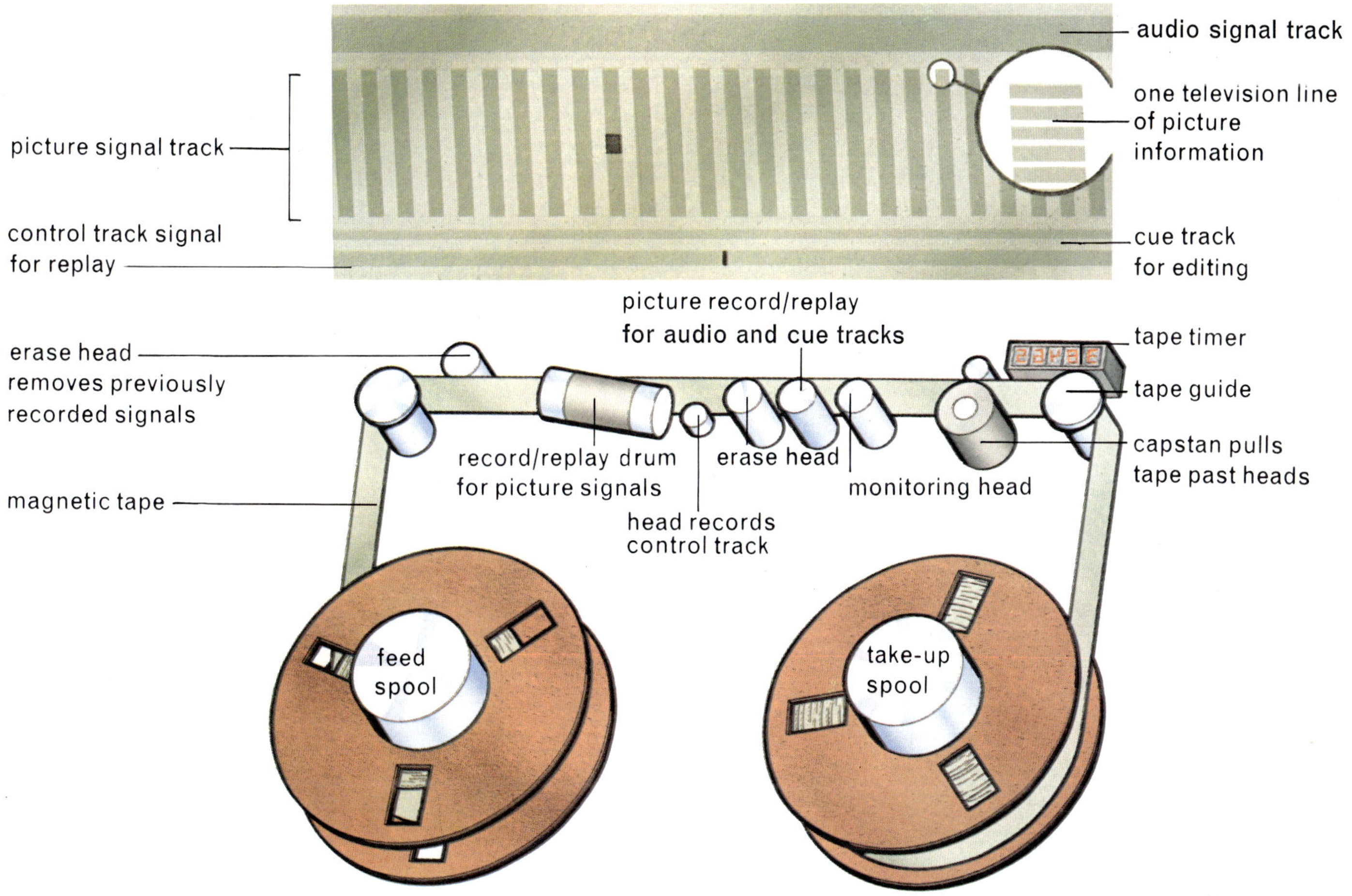
audio signal track
one television line of picture information
picture signal track
control track signal for replay
cue track for editing
picture record/replay
for audio and cue tracks
erase head removes previously recorded signals
tape timer
tape guide
capstan pulls tape past heads
record/replay drum for picture signals
erase head
monitoring head
magnetic tape
head records control track
feed spool
take-up spool

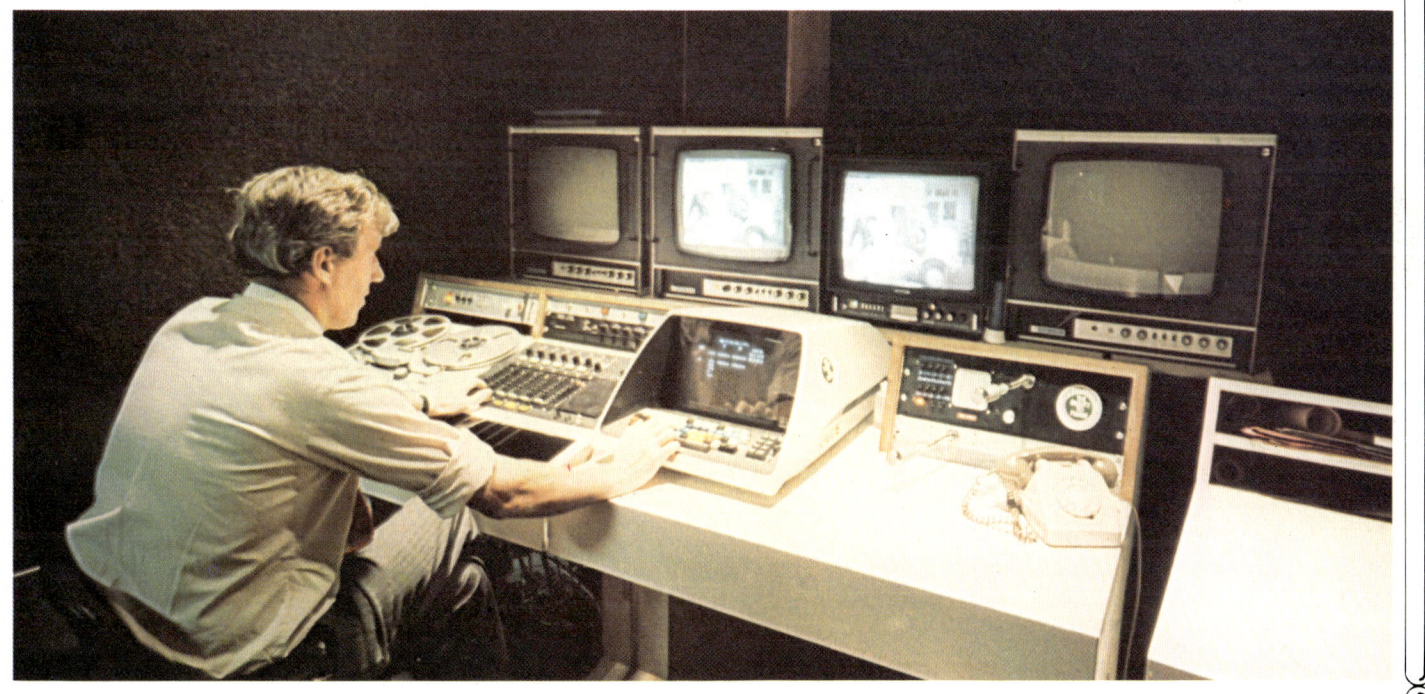

Video tricks

TV can play tricks on viewers. One person may play two people at the same time, talking to each other. Real actors might appear to be acting with cartoon characters in cartoon backgrounds. News film of explosions, meetings or other events magically shows up on what seems to be a blank wall behind a newscaster's head. How does it happen?

Two at once

All these tricks are possible because two or more pictures can appear on the screen at the same time even though they come from different sources. The color of one picture triggers the signal of another picture. The system that does this is called chroma-key ('key' for short) and it enables two or more separate pictures to be merged into one for some amazing effects.

Tricks with chroma-key

Camera 1

The dotted line shows the shot the camera is taking of this scene.

Camera 2

The picture that appears on viewers' TV screens.

A key color is chosen as a background—usually blue, since it isn't like skin tones. One camera focuses on, for example, some dancers in front of this background while at the same time a second camera focuses on a pop-up book. The tubes in the first camera are continuously scanning the dancers and the blue background. When the scanning beam hits the blue background, the blue signal is at its strongest and triggers a switch in a chroma-key switcher. The pop-up book from the second camera is substituted in place of the blue background and viewers see the dancers as if they were dancing in the book.

38

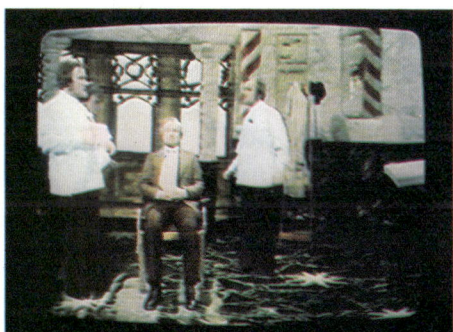

A magic carpet
For the 'flying' carpet trick they use a background of clouds and overlay them with a cartoon drawing of the carpet on a blue background and a shot of the man sitting on a blue floor. The carpet disappears by switching to a single overlay of the man and clouds. Finally, the man 'falls' out of the sky by tilting up the camera.

Through the mirror
A woman appears to walk through a magic mirror. But it is a fake. She actually walks through a blue flat containing a doorway, which is hung with a curtain made from strips of blue felt. The doorway is the same size as the mirror on the set and when one shot is overlaid on the other, the performer appears to walk through the mirror. Another shot shows her on the other side looking back at the magic mirror.

One man plays four parts
To create this trick they start with a shot of the set, then combine it with a picture of the actor standing against a blue background. He becomes two men by overlaying another picture of him against a blue background on top of the first recording on the videotape and so on until the group is built up.

Take 1!

Film cameras, tape recorders and even the lights can run off batteries and operate in places far from electricity outlets. So for nature programs and documentaries made in remote parts of the world, film is still the best way to take pictures. But putting the film together can take a long time and miniature remote units are replacing film for stories that are needed quickly, such as news, or for drama inserts, because of better picture quality.

One at a time

Unlike TV, where each shot follows the one before in the story order, film shots are taken one at a time. They are rarely taken in the right order and many more shots are filmed than will be used in the final film. Sometimes filmmakers will shoot a scene, or part of a scene, over and over again because it's not right. Every time the camera starts up, the slate★ is clapped and the camera takes a picture of the numbers on it. Each part of a scene has a number, called a *slate* number, to identify it, and a *take* number which shows whether it's the first or tenth time that it has been shot!

The slate always has the name of the production, the director, the slate number and the take number on it.

The slate's job

The sound and the picture are recorded *separately*—the pictures go onto film and the sound onto magnetic tape. Keeping the sound and picture together in the final film is called synchronization (sync for short). Every time the camera starts,

someone holds up the slate in front of it. He holds the top of it open and then brings it sharply down on the bottom part. The camera films this moment and the microphone picks up the sound of the clap. There is now one film frame

showing the moment at which the slate closes together with a piece of tape with the clap recorded on it. The film editor matches the first frame showing the closed slate with the sound of the clap to put sound and picture in sync.

Fitting the pieces together

At the end of filming, the film is sent to a film laboratory, where it is processed overnight. The laboratory keeps the precious negative from which positive copies can be made and sends one positive copy to the film editor. The editor cuts it up and joins it together again to make a guide called a cutting copy. The laboratory cuts the negative to match this cutting copy. A print of the cut negative is the completed film.

Looking at a comic strip like this one will help you see how a film is made. Each box in the comic strip story is like a shot in the film. It tells one bit of the story. Notice how from one picture box to another the artist draws the scene from a different angle or in bigger detail or from further away. A film is made up from shots in a similar way. The editor puts the film shots in the best order to tell the story.

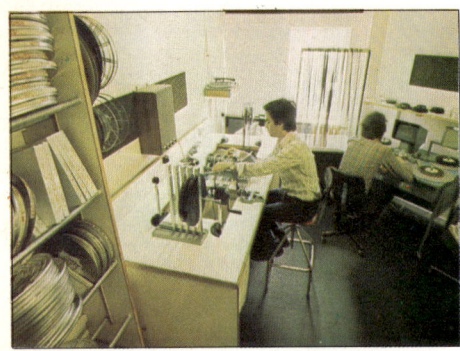

This is a cutting room. There may be 30 hours of film to make a one-hour program, so to find shots quickly, the film is filed.

2. The film director and the film editor look at the film on an editing machine. They decide on a rough shape for the film and make a selection of shots they think they will use.

1. The sound is transferred from magnetic tape onto magnetic film so that it can be cut to match the picture. The sound and picture are put onto the synchronizer. The picture and sound of the slate are then matched for each shot and marked to identify them.

3. The film editor cuts the film and joins together the selections with transparent tape. The rest of the

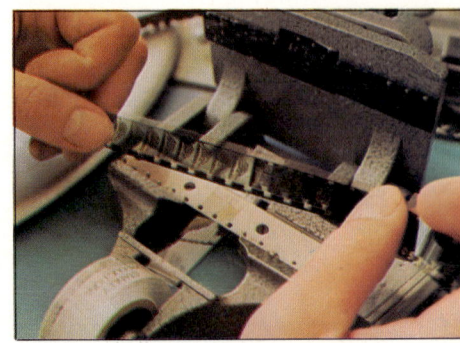

film is carefully filed away in cans, in case the editor wants to make changes and use any of it.

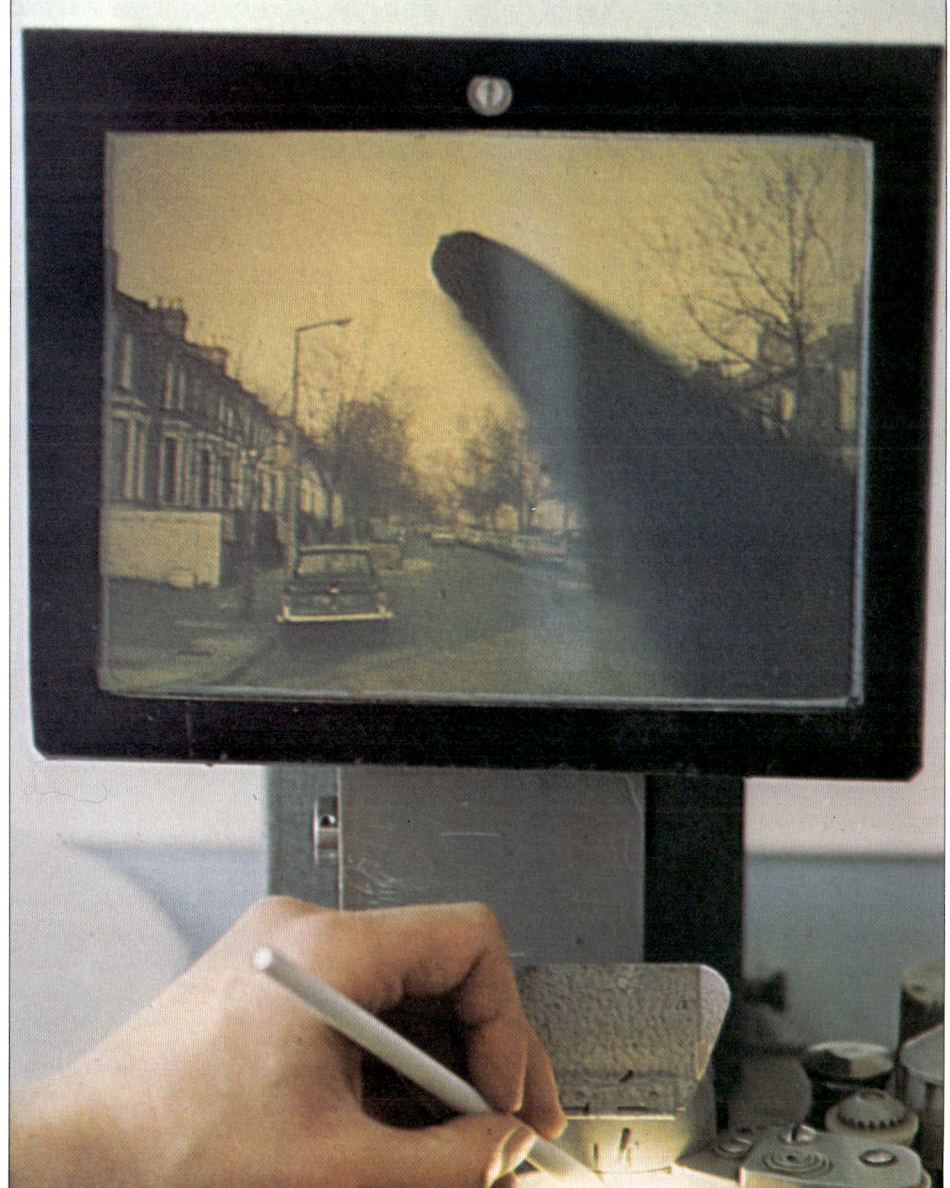

4. The director and editor then view the rough assembly of shots and decide whether the arrangement is right. The editor then keeps on making changes until they are satisfied with the film.

Matching the sound
5. The soundtrack is usually a mixture of speech, music and sound effects, such as footsteps, car noises and wind. These sounds are all kept separate from one another by placing blank film, called spacing, in between each one. Where several sounds are going to be heard together, each one is put on a separate reel. Spacing keeps the sound in sync with the picture.

Dubbing chart
The editor prepares a dubbing chart like the one above for the dubbing engineer to use as a guide. It tells him when and where all the different sounds come.
In the dubbing room, he plays the reels of sound with the picture and matches them together. The pictures and sound for the final film are each on a single reel with no joins.

43

Film tricks

Everything you see in a film is not always as it appears. Filmmakers use various tricks to fool your eyes.

Spot the trick
Some tricks are achieved by using a particular type of film or camera, others are created by using models.

Next time you watch a film on TV, see how many of these tricks you can spot. Look for scenes where you suspect models have been used—sinking ships, crashing cars and exploding planes are some examples.

Editing makes it seem real
Some film effects are created at the editing stage. Shots filmed separately, and even out of order, are joined together to make an action look as if it happened all at one time. Sound effects are added to heighten the action.

Shot 1. A real man, just about to fall through a window, is filmed from inside a room.

Shot 2. A dummy, exactly the same size as the man and wearing identical clothes, falls from the window and is filmed from the ground.

Shot 3. The real man, lying on the pavement and pretending to be dead, is filmed from on the ground.

Editing. The three different shots are joined together so that it looks as if the falling and landing are continuous, and sounds of thuds, screams and sirens are added.

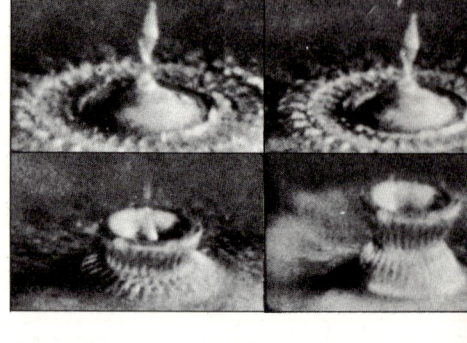

Slowing down the action
If film is shot at a faster speed than usual, it enables people to see details which normally happen too fast for the eye to see. The film is projected at the normal 24 frames per second so that the

Speeding up the action
A flower may take days to open from bud to full bloom. If a camera is set up to shoot one

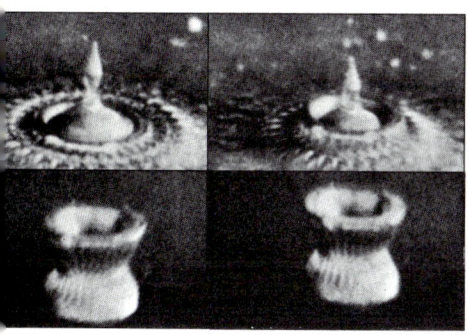

action appears to be slowed down. If this drop of mercury had been shot at normal speed you would only see a drop and then a splash. In these pictures, filmed at high speed, you can see in great detail the changing shape of the splash.

frame every two hours, on film the flower will appear to open in a few seconds. This is called time lapse filming.

Models that trick
It would be too expensive to build a dummy city for a fire scene. Instead, a whole town is built in miniature and set on fire. The film crew then take realistic shots of the blaze! Models are also used for shipwrecks and science fiction.

Juggling the shots
An editor can juggle camera shots and tell a story in one of several ways. Look at these two versions of a story. They use the same pictures in different orders. Which is the more dramatic? In the first, the quiet of the churchyard is disturbed by a coffin opening. It's Dracula! He crosses the moonlit field in search of a victim, who is sound asleep, unaware of her fate. The door of her bedroom opens... In the second, a woman sleeps peacefully. In the churchyard all seems quiet, too. Or is it? The coffin creaks, opens and a hand emerges. A silhouette flits across the night sky. Who can it be? The door opens and Dracula is revealed!

Tell a story
Can you arrange these pictures in an order which tells a story? This is what a film editor does. There are several different ways to do it. Decide what sound effects and speech you would put in.

Turning film into TV

Many TV programs, such as movies, wildlife documentaries and cartoons, are made on film.

Turning film into TV
Before they can be broadcast, films have to be turned into electrical signals, so they are run through a machine called a telecine★ at the television studio. Some telecine machines turn slides into a TV picture for use on news and educational programs.

Straight at a TV camera
The simplest telecine system uses an ordinary film projector which shines the moving pictures onto a small TV camera. The camera scans each frame of film for a fraction of a second and converts it into an electrical signal in the normal way (see page 8). A more sophisticated telecine is the 'flying spot' machine.

A flying spot telecine
To turn a film into TV, light from a cathode ray tube scans each film frame, passes through it and is turned into red, blue and green electrical signals.

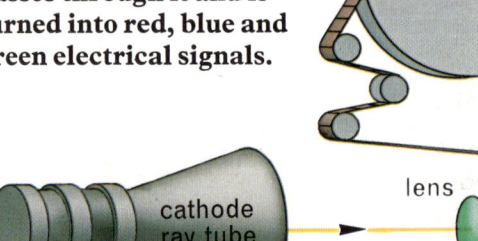

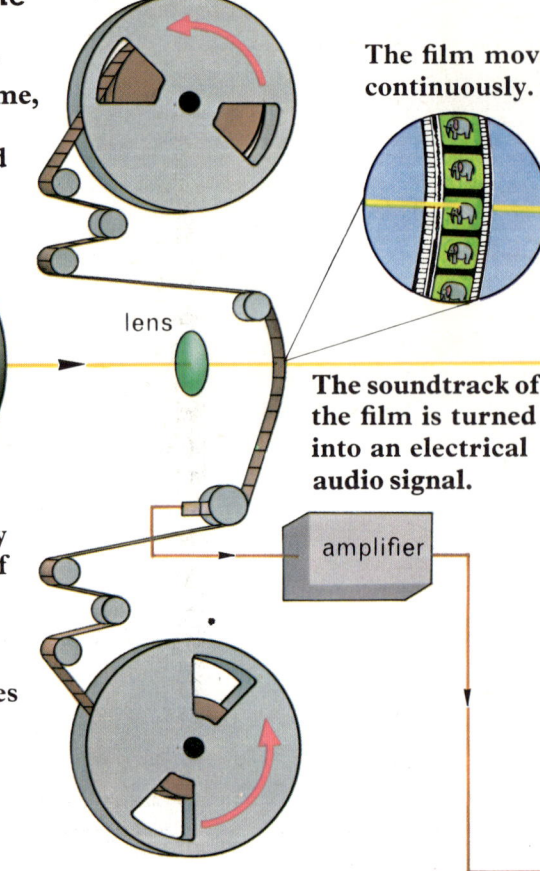

The film moves continuously.

The flying spot
This cathode ray tube has a beam of electricity which scans the front of the tube, producing a spot of light that 'flies' so fast across the front of the tube that it makes a pattern of lines called a 'raster'.
A lens focuses light from the raster onto the film.

The soundtrack of the film is turned into an electrical audio signal.

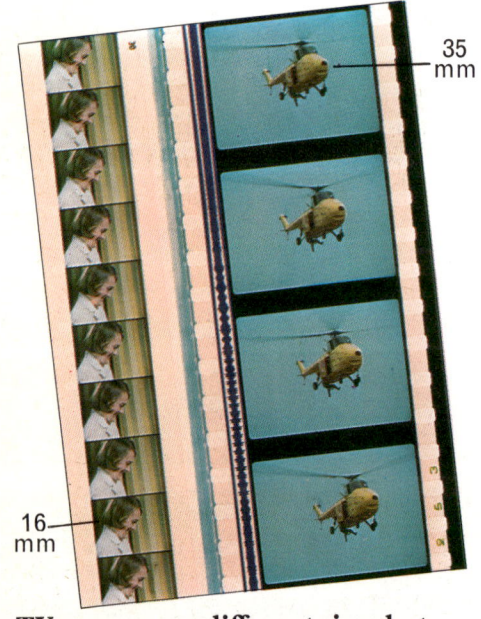

35 mm
16 mm

TV screens are different sizes but they all show pictures of the same ratio—3 deep by 4 across. 16 mm and 35 mm film frames have a larger picture ratio than 3 by 4, so that you see slightly less of the picture when you watch it on TV than you would at the movies. But the difference is so small that it is impossible to notice.

Cinemascope
Showing cinemascope film on TV is more of a problem because the picture on each frame is distorted sideways so that everything looks long and narrow. (In theaters, the projector has a special lens to correct the pictures.) The telecine machine corrects the pictures by altering the size of the screen of light which scans each frame of the film.

There are two ways of doing this. You can tell quite easily which way has been used.
1. The flying spot can scan the full width of the film frame. When this is done you will see blank areas left above and below the pictures because the full cinemascope picture has a different ratio from the TV picture.

Light from the raster scans the film. After passing through the film, the light is split into its red, green and blue components. More light passes through the pale parts of the frames than the dark parts.

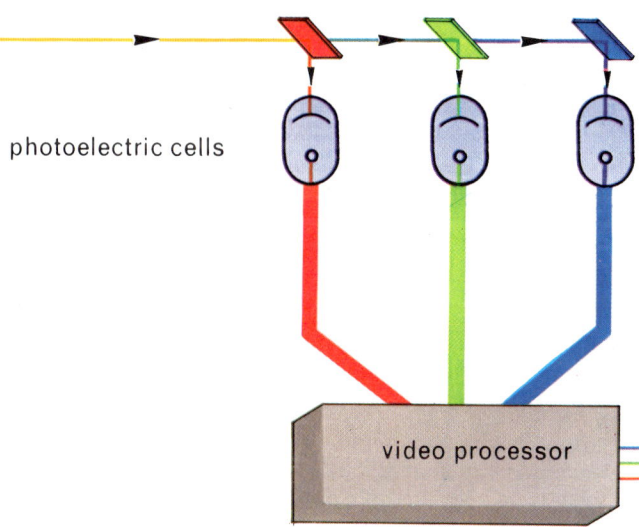

photoelectric cells

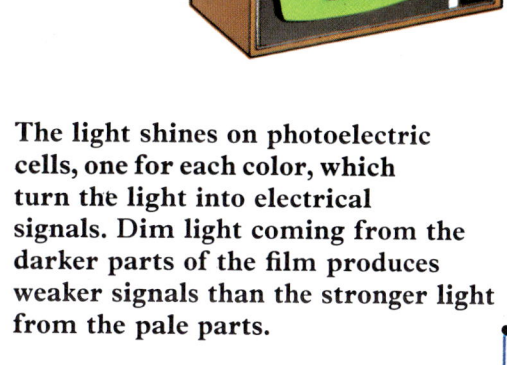

The light shines on photoelectric cells, one for each color, which turn the light into electrical signals. Dim light coming from the darker parts of the film produces weaker signals than the stronger light from the pale parts.

The three electrical signals are combined electrically in the video processor to produce a combined picture signal which is broadcast on carrier waves to TV sets.

picture signal

audio signal

video processor

2. The flying spot screen can be matched to the height of the film, and only scan half the width. The screen of light can be moved from side to side across the film frames to avoid losing any important action. When this method is used, you will see complete titles and the picture looks stretched lengthways, just as it does on each frame of film.

A telecine machine takes several seconds to run up to speed before the beginning of a film. A length of film, known as a leader, is spliced to the front of the film. This has film footage numbers on it. It is run through the machine shortly before the film starts. If the cue to start the machine is wrongly timed, you may see the leader numbers on your screen.

Many films are more than one reel long, so two telecine machines are used, one after the other. There is a mark on the corner of the film, a few feet before the end of each reel. This warns the telecine operator that it is time to change to the other machine. Look for this mark, called a cue, in the top right-hand corner of the screen.

A frame at a time

Cartoons may look simple but they require a lot of hard work and imagination. The cartoonist makes thousands of drawings, each one different from the last. These are filmed in order, a frame at a time, with a rostrum camera (a camera designed to look down upon the cartoons), and when they are projected, at 24 frames per second, the still drawings appear to move. This process is called animation. It takes a long time to make an animated film. Twelve people can take over a week to make a 30-second film.

Adding real sound
Sounds for animated films are added separately. Voices, explosions, crowd noises and so on are dubbed to synchronize with the picture.

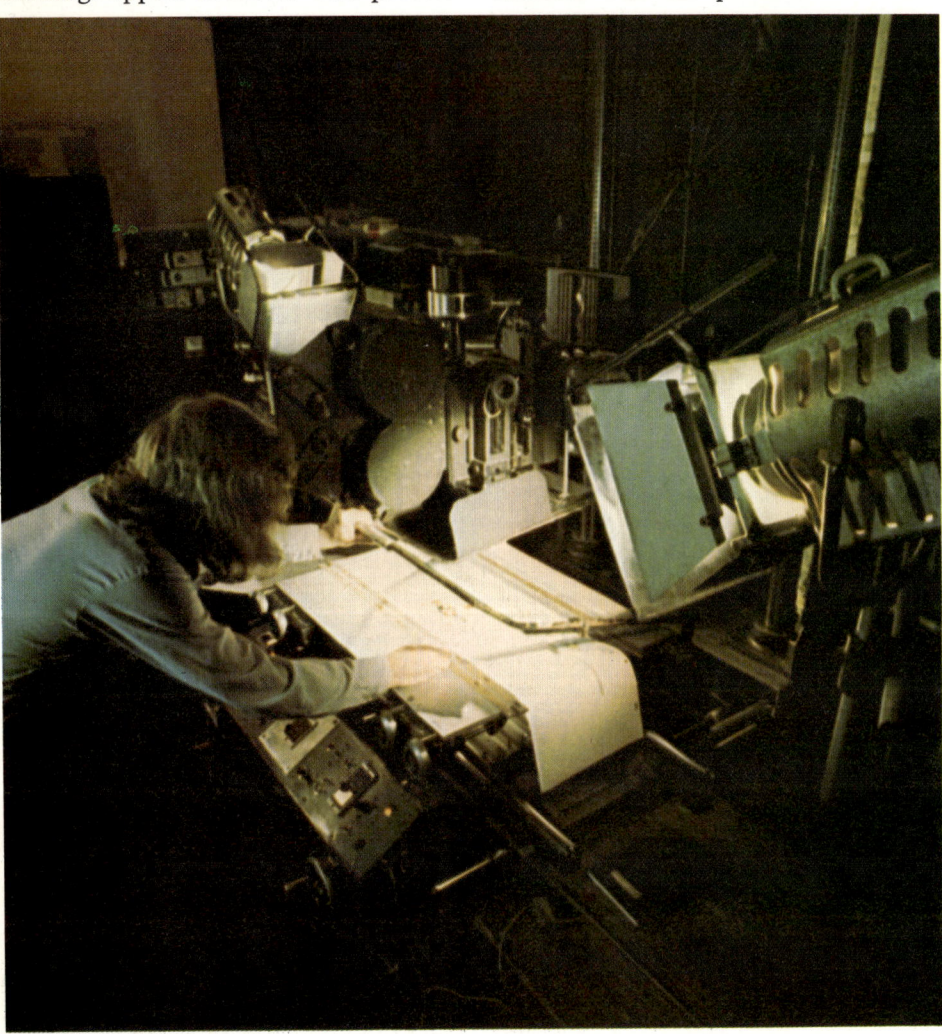

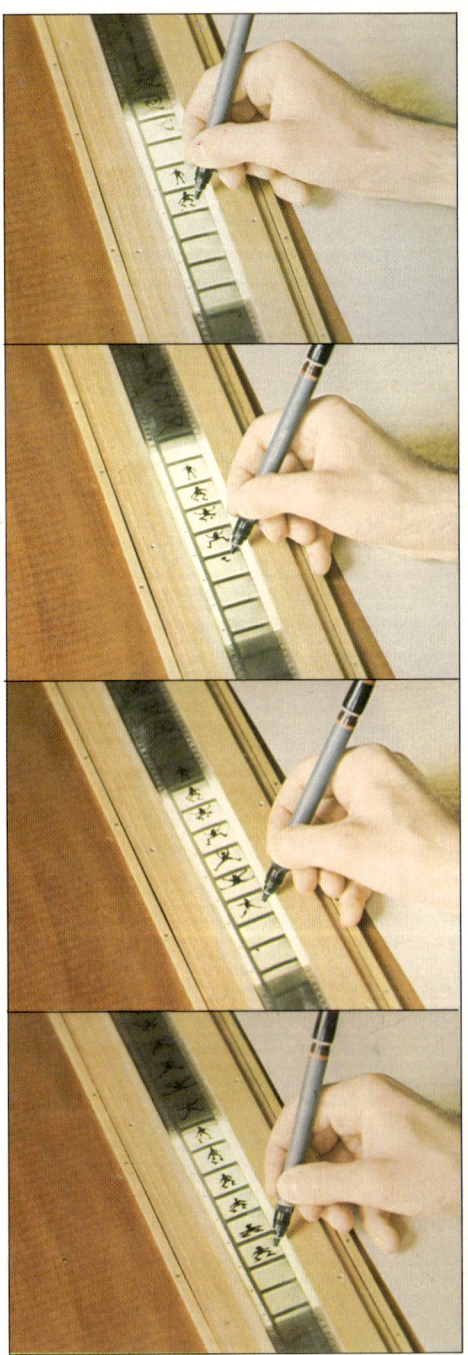

Rostrum camera
It is easiest to film drawings laid flat, so an animation camera is usually mounted facing downward onto them. Since even the tiniest shake would be noticeable, the camera is fixed to a strong metal stand, which holds it rigid. The operator pins the drawings to a movable table and places sheets of glass over them to keep them flat. He then turns hand wheels at the front of the table to move the drawings into different positions under the camera. Lamps of equal strength light the drawing and are never moved once filming has begun. When everything is ready, the operator presses a switch on the panel in front of him to work the camera. The film in the rostrum camera can move forward or backward one frame at a time.

Drawing onto film
A few cartoonists draw directly onto film. First they dissolve the emulsion on the film, leaving it clear and transparent. Then they draw a miniature picture on each frame of film with pen and ink.

48

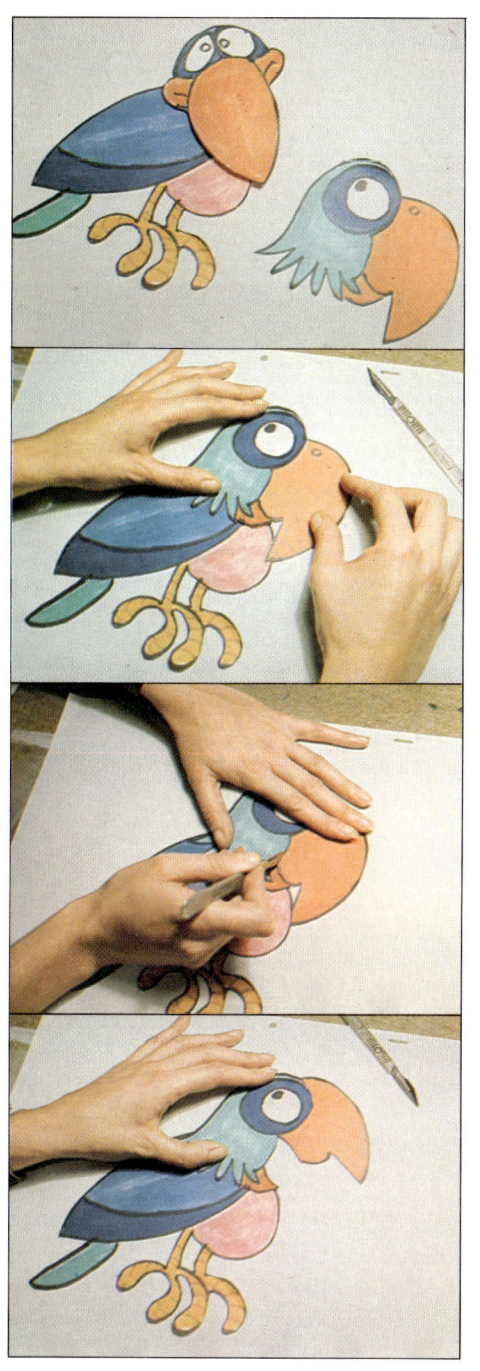

Cutout models
Other artists use cutout paper models. A cameraman films the cutout model in one position, then moves it slightly and films it again. Characters are often cut out in several sizes with different hands or heads so that each one can be used for a particular shot, such as a wide shot or a close-up.

Puppets
Some films are made using puppets. They often have wire or metal joints that can move, but which will stay in place once they have been set for filming. The puppets are filmed thousands of times in a slightly different position for each frame. When the film is run, the puppets appear to move.

Cels
One of the most complicated ways of animating is by using cels. These are transparent sheets of cellophane and the drawings are painted on them. The cels are put on top of one another and filmed together. This is the method used when characters appear to move in front of painted backgrounds.

Gathering the news

The news of the day, gathered from all over the world on film or tape or live by satellite, is transmitted live to TV sets all over the country.

Bringing in the news

The steady voice of the newscaster gives no idea of the news team's hectic day. These people, who are rarely seen on the screen, spend long hours preparing the news in time for the program. Early in the morning, a domestic news editor investigates the national news items to follow up, while a foreign news editor catches up on stories from abroad. Newswriters read all the stories that come in from news agencies. Most of them are thrown away, but the important stories are passed to the producer. Then correspondents with particular interests (political, diplomatic, scientific) prepare specialist stories. To weave all the various bits of news into a program, the executive producer holds a conference to discuss the items, to decide how long each one should be and in what order they should be shown.

Reporters and camera crews are sent out to record on-the-spot news. Reporters prepare film narrations and the introductions to news items, and photo librarians find suitable photographs to go with a story. The scriptwriters cut stories to the right length, and finally the typist taps out the narrations on long sheets to be then fitted on the teleprompter.

Half an hour before the program, the newscaster and the people in the control room have a rehearsal. Films are put on telecine and tapes on the videotape machines. Now everything is ready.

All the news of the day is read and sorted out in this newsroom.

Here is the news!

The news has to fit into a tight time schedule, starting and finishing at just the right second. This means that sometimes the news team has to shorten stories even while they are on the air or drop them altogether. And if a bulletin comes through, they must be able to slot it in. The newscaster has to be prepared for anything! Here is a typical mixture of news that might be shown in a day. The newscaster's narration links all the stories.

A remote broadcast transmits, live to the studio, a report about a forest fire sweeping across the countryside.

A satellite transmits live the blast-off into orbit of a space probe.

Still photographs accompany a story about a mineworkers' meeting.

There are separate newsdesks for each news program of the day.

The executive producer has the final say in selecting the stories.

Useful background information is stored in these archives.

A science correspondent in the studio describes the development of a miniature TV.

A sudden bulletin comes in about the attempted assassination of a famous politician.

A telecine machine runs some film of a long-distance running race. A courier has rushed this to the studio earlier in the day. Laboratories in the news department processed the film in less than 30 minutes. An editor cut it and a scriptwriter wrote a narration for it just in time for the news.

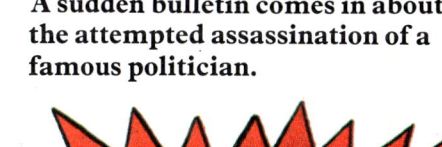

Here is the news

When the news is on the air a newscaster's job is a lonely one. For as long as it lasts he or she must keep going.

Given the go-ahead

From the moment the director gives him the cue to start and he begins reading from the teleprompter★, the newscaster has to take any film breakdowns, changes of story and last-minute bulletins in his stride. He must read every word clearly and at a steady pace. It is no wonder that viewers can sometimes hear the relief in the newscaster's voice as he says, '*And that's the way it is.*'

★ **How a teleprompter works**
To viewers it looks as if the newscaster knows the news by heart, but he doesn't. He reads the script from a screen which is held below the lens of the camera. The newscaster looks at the camera and, therefore, the viewer straight in the eye and reads the script at the same time. The words have been typed, very large, four to five words to a line so that they are easy to read.
The prompting machine operator sits at a desk in another part of the studio, out of sight of the cameras, and moves the paper at the reading speed of the newscaster.
A narrow roll of paper holds the typed script.

A closed-circuit TV camera continually scans the script as it moves under the lens.
The camera sends an image of the script to the monitor which is underneath the lens of the studio camera.

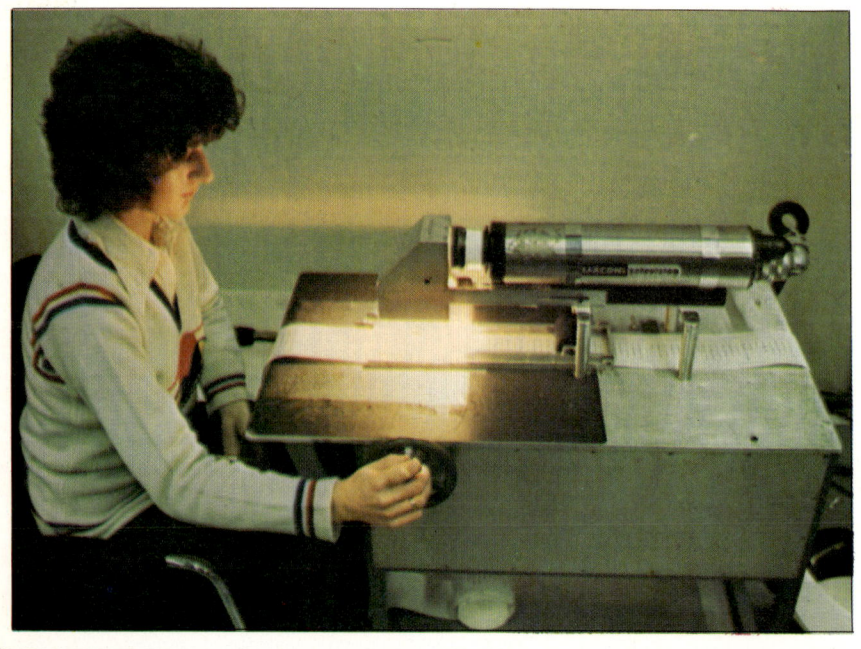

The director's voice alerts the cameras and the stage manager, whose job is to cue the newscaster.

A special correspondent waits for his cue.

This TV monitor shows the newscaster film and tape inserts in the news.

There are two telephones on the newsdesk. One connects the newscaster to the production control room; the other is an outside line, so that he can talk to roving reporters.

This blue screen is for chroma-key pictures (see page 38).

The newscaster wears an earpiece through which he receives instructions from the control room.

The newscaster has a script to read from and can use the prompting machine as an aid.

The teleprompter operator sits at a machine here.

This monitor shows the studio what picture is being transmitted.

Landmarks in TV

A lot has happened in television since John Logie Baird, the Scottish inventor, and the American, Charles Francis Jenkins, experimented with black and white flickering pictures over fifty years ago. At first, pictures could be sent only over short distances but technical improvements have changed this. Today, pictures can be sent instantly across the world and even from the Moon and Mars.

Smaller and cheaper

Now the TV industry is making smaller, cheaper and more sensitive equipment. There are cameras, sound recorders and videomachines light enough for one person to carry and take TV pictures. Some TV cameras can even 'see' in the dark.

1925: Baird invents a camera that splits pictures mechanically.
1928: First transmission of pictures across the Atlantic.
1929: 30-line Baird system is transmitted by BBC for half an hour per day.
1932: Zworykin makes the iconoscope camera tube in the U.S.
1935: In England, Marconi-EMI announce that they can produce a picture with 405 scanning lines.
1937: Dumont manufactures first TV sets in the U.S. and transmits experimentally.
1941: First commercial TV in the U.S. over WNBT in New York.
1951: First color television program is put out by Columbia Broadcasting System (CBS).
1961: First live Moscow to Europe broadcast shows Gagarin returning to Moscow after the first manned space orbit.
1962: Telstar, the first telecommunications satellite to carry transatlantic TV signals, is launched.
1967: First regular color TV transmission in Europe by the BBC.
1969: First live TV pictures from the moon, with 723 million viewers.
1976: Worldwide transmission of the Montreal Olympics.

Baird used this early camera to transmit pictures of a ventriloquist's dummy over a short distance, with 30-line vertical scanning.

Mechanical mirrordrum cameras like this were made as late as 1936.

One of the first remote broadcasts was the 1939 Derby horserace.

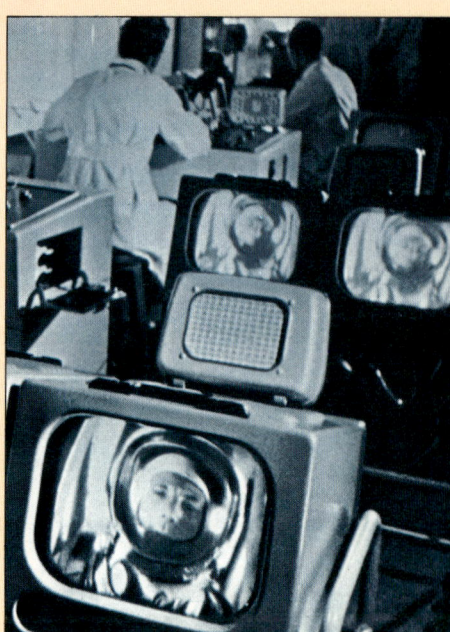

Gagarin was monitored during his flight. He orbited at only 344 km (203 miles) away from the Earth's surface, so there was no delay between sending and receiving the TV pictures. But TV pictures from the Viking space probes on Mars took four minutes to reach Earth because of the immense distances that the carrier waves had to travel.

One of Baird's original televisors. The wheel-shaped mechanical scanner is at the back. A powerful lens behind the screen on the right magnified the picture.

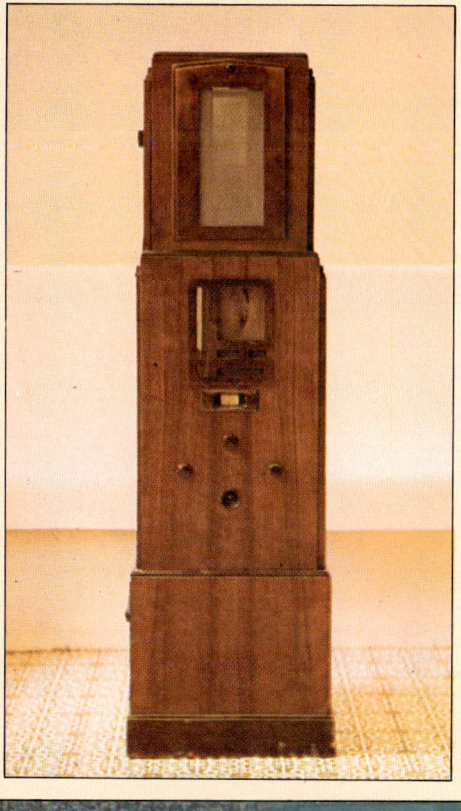

▲The iconoscope camera tube was the first which scanned pictures electronically rather than mechanically, with 405 scanning lines.

◀A mirrordrum receiver—an early TV set—with 30-line vertical scanning, based on the Baird principle. You would have seen pictures like the one on page 5 on this screen.

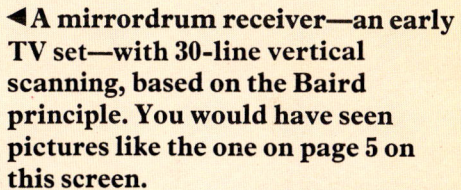

Telstar (above) was the first satellite to transmit TV pictures. Much more sophisticated telecommunications satellites transmitted the 1976 Olympics to 450 million viewers.

Not just for fun

TV is much more than a home entertainment. There are now very few kinds of work where TV is not used, and by the time you are in a job, it will be even more widespread.

Mini TV cameras

This doesn't mean that large cameras, studios and control rooms are found in every factory or office. The cameras used in industry, medicine, aviation and so on are small—often not much larger than a home movie camera. They are easily carried and can be mounted on a wall or ceiling. They're also fitted on to spy-in-the-sky satellites, which allow one country to find out information about another. The development of miniature, complicated electronic circuits gave TV cameras this great flexibility. But the picture signals they produce are not always sent through the air. Often they can travel only along cables, which restricts their use to linking up different parts of a building or a town. The system is called closed-circuit television. It has this name because the pictures aren't broadcast to the general public, but are confined to the areas or rooms linked by cables.

Closed-circuit TV is a good way to guard a vast factory.

A remote control camera monitors traffic on a busy highway. Traffic controllers, watching on TV screens, take action if they see congestion.

Industry uses closed-circuit TV to check on the making of products.

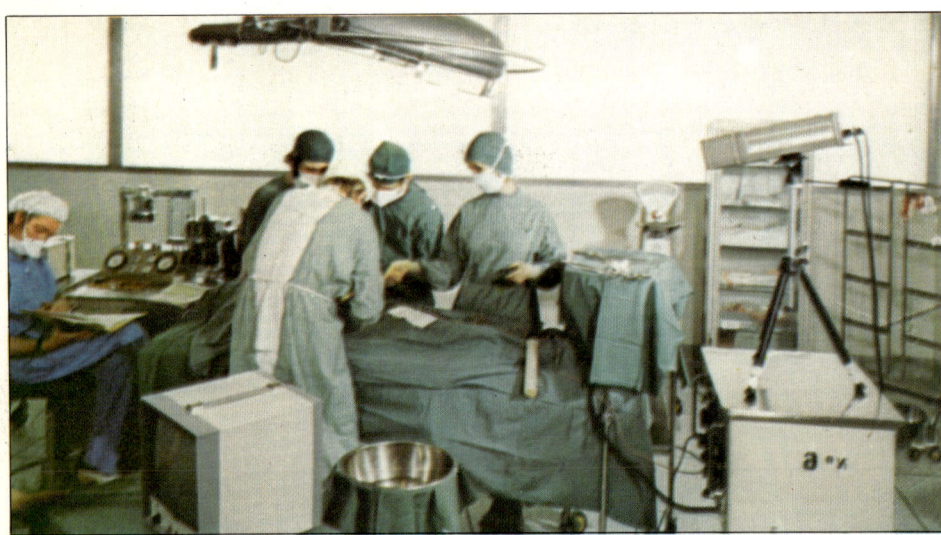

A TV camera follows every step of an operation in the theater, and medical students learn by watching a TV set in another room.

Patients in intensive care can be watched without risk of infection.

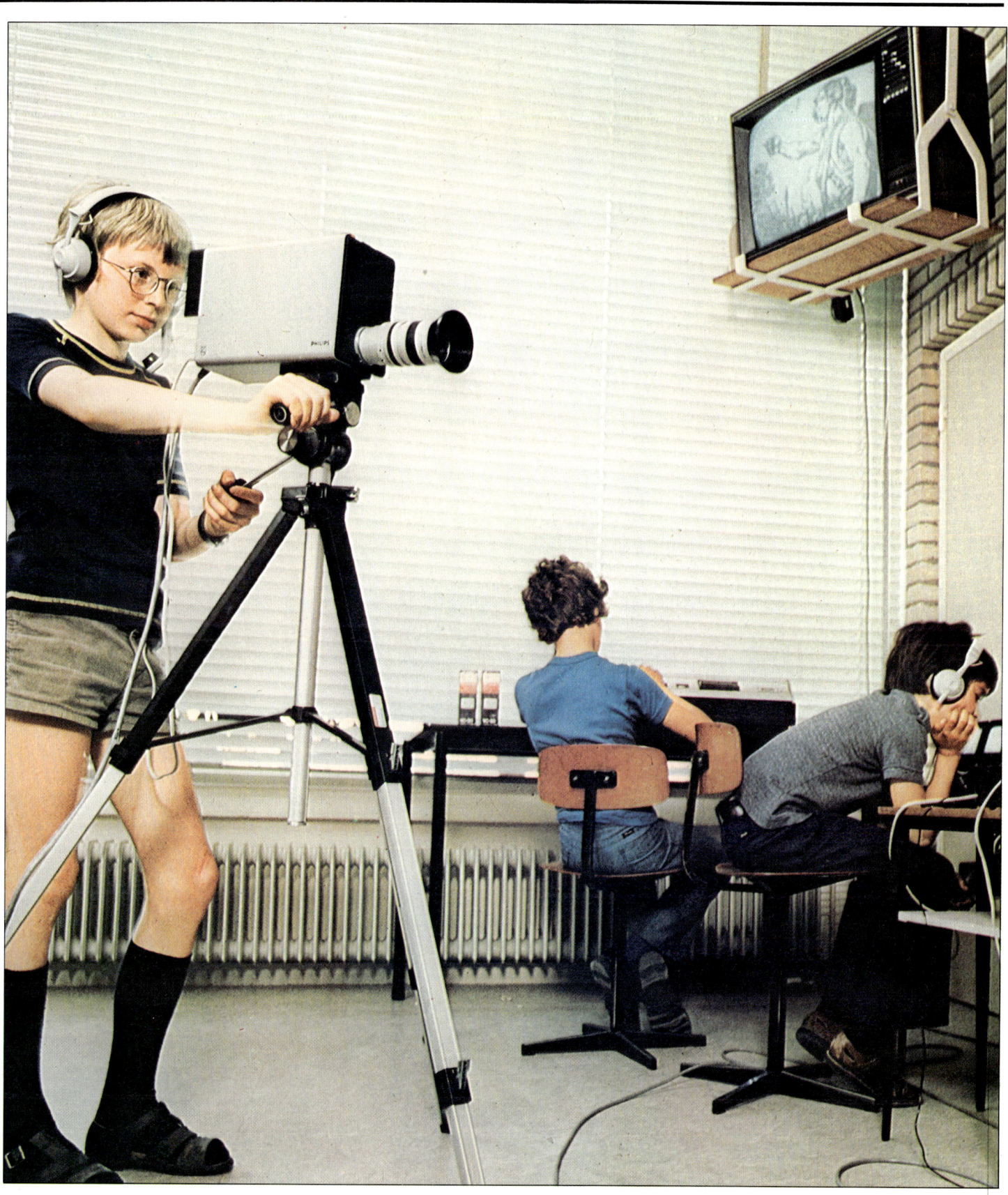

Pupils use closed-circuit TV equipment themselves, to produce their own school news reports and to record lessons or performances. Teachers can record craft or sports lessons and replay them in class.

More and more possibilities

What do you think tomorrow's world will be like and how will television have changed? Certainly, TV sets will offer more instant information by using push-button codes to select sports results, travel timetables and many other things. TV screens will become big, flat panels on walls. And you will probably make your own TV programs with miniature equipment and send video cassettes to friends overseas, instead of letters. Can you predict other uses for TV?

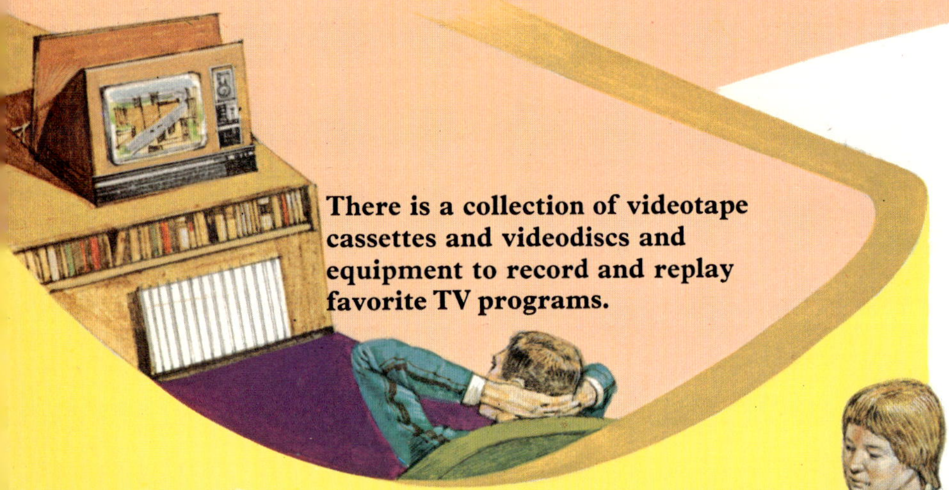

There is a collection of videotape cassettes and videodiscs and equipment to record and replay favorite TV programs.

With a compact camera, microphone and videotape recorder, a boy sets off to record a carnival. He carries a miniature TV set so he can watch a program while he's out.

If everyone is out, an outside telephone caller can use pushbutton codes to leave a message on a TV screen which is part of the telephone system.

A large, flat screen on the wall shows TV pictures and all sorts of instant information.

Two children play one of the many telegames that they can plug into their TV screen.

In the kitchen, a viewer presses a button on the TV and it prints out a recipe for a dish which has just been shown on the screen.

Thousands of programs are stored at a central video library. To select one, a viewer drops a coin in a slot and dials a code.

Contributors

Our thanks go to the following for their help in preparing this book: Bura and Hardwick Animation, Darling and Wood Television (Norwich), Document Film Services, Derek Dodd, Mike Fox, Bob Godfrey Studio, Marika Hegerty, Adam, Pippa and Sarah Humphries, IBA Broadcasting Gallery, Independent Television News, John Laurence (ABC News), Alan McIlwaine (Rank Cintel), Eric Mival, Jupiter Sen, Thames Television, Neil Thomson, Kevin Woolridge. The book was prepared in consultation with John Goss, Stewart Marshall, Derek Dodd and others of BBC Television.

Photographs

Barry Breckon, page number 23. BBC Copyright Photographs 1, 2, 3, 21, 22, 24, 25, 34, 35, 44, 45, 54. British Aircraft Corporation 14. Bura and Hardwick Animation 44-5. Cable and Wireless 15. Chubb Alarms 56. Colorsport 15, 55. Courtesy of EMI Elstree Studios 46, 47. Crown Copyright. Science Museum, London 54. EMI Sound and Vision 56. Mike Freeman 14-5. John Hadland (Photographic Instrumentation) 44-5. Henson Associates Incorporated 5, 39. ITN inside front cover, 28, 50, 51. Ken Kirkwood 16, 29, 31. Marconi-Elliott Avionic Systems 56. Novosti Press Agency 54. Post Office Telecommunications 55. Pye Business Communications 57. Radio Rentals 5. Rediffusion Industrial Services 56. Phil Sayer 5, 16, 20, 21, 22, 23, 28, 34, 35, 36, 37, 39, 40-1, 42, 43, 48, 49, 50, 51, 54, 55. Raghubir Singh/The John Hillelson Agency 14. Shaun Skelley, inside front cover, 49. Thames Television 23. Yorkshire Television 60.

Illustrations

Terry Pastor: Front cover. Bura and Hardwick Animation 49. Roy Castle 40. Ken Cox 4, 5, 9, 29, 44, 45. Derek D 20, 21, 23. Richard Draper 10-1, 52-3. Joan Ellacott 22. Bob G Studio 48, 49. Tony Hannaford, front cover, 13, 16, 33, 38. Trevor 8-9, Richard Hook 7, 30, 31, 32-3, Frank Kennard 6-7, 12-3. Paul Sa 42-3. John Thompson Associates Jim Wilkinson 11, 37. Joseph Wrigh 50-1.

INDEX

A
amplifier 17, 46
animation 48, 49
antenna 6, 7, 10, 12, 13, 14, 15
archive 51
assistant cameraman 41
associate director 18, 30
audio engineer 11, 30, 32
audio signal 6, 7, 12, 17, 37, 46, 47

B
backdrop 23
Baird, John Logie 54, 55
'barndoor' 34
battery 11, 14
BBC 54
boom dolly 18, 32
boom operator 18, 32
bulletin 50, 51, 52

C
cable 10, 13, 56
camera card 28
cameraman 7, 19, 28, 29, 41, 49
camera script 31
camera shot 10, 28, 29, 30, 31, 44, 45, 49
camera tube 7, 8, 9, 54, 55
'cans' 19, 28
carpenter 22, 23
carrier wave 12, 13, 14, 47, 54
cartoon 48
cathode ray tube 46
cel 49
cellophane 9, 49
chroma-key 38, 53
cinemascope film 46, 47
closed-circuit TV 52, 56, 57
close-up 29, 31, 49
color 8, 9, 16
Columbia Broadcasting System 54
control room 7, 10, 11, 12, 51
correspondent 50, 51, 52
costume designer 22
cue 10, 18, 47, 52
cut 31
cutting room 42

D
dissolve 31
director 18, 20, 21, 30, 41, 42, 43, 52
dubbing chart 43
dummy 44

E
earphones 19, 28
earpiece 52
editing 36, 42, 44
editor 42, 43, 45, 50, 51
electrical signal 7, 8, 9, 33, 46
electricity beam 8, 9, 17, 46
electromagnet 9
electronic circuit 56
engineer 11
engineer in charge 30
executive producer 50
experiments and projects 4, 5, 9, 16, 34, 45

F
faceplate 17
film 26, 40, 41, 42, 44, 46
film editor 40, 42, 45
film projector 46
floor manager 21
flying spot machine 46
focus 8, 9, 28
frame 44, 46, 47, 48

G
generator 6